The
Faith-Filled
Grandmother

The Faith-Filled Grandmother

PROMISES, PRAYERS & PRACTICAL ADVICE FOR TODAY

Teresa Kindred

Good Books

New York, New York

Good Books books may be purchased in bulk at special discounts for sales promotion, corporate gifts, fund-raising, or educational purposes. Special editions can also be created to specifications. For details, contact the Special Sales Department, Good Books, 307 West 36th Street, 11th Floor, New York, NY 10018 or info@skyhorsepublishing.com.

Good Books in an imprint of Skyhorse Publishing, Inc.®, a Delaware corporation.

Visit our website at www.goodbooks.com.

10 9 8 7 6 5 4 3

Library of Congress Cataloging-in-Publication Data is available on file.

Cover design by Qualcom
Cover photo credit iStockphoto

Print ISBN: 978-1-68099-429-2
Ebook ISBN: 978-1-68099-430-8

Printed in China

Table of Contents

Introduction

"What sort of problems do today's grandmothers face? What are her hopes and fears? How do grandmothers handle family issues that threaten peace within their families?"

About ten years ago, I started a blog named NanaHood. I chose that name because I believe NanaHood is the second half of the motherhood journey. Over the years, I added on social media accounts, and today NanaHood's Facebook page has a following of close to 50,000 grandmothers from all over the world. To find the answers to the questions above, I turned to these grandmothers. My questions reached over 18,000 women, and hundreds of them responded. They opened up their hearts and shared their joys, sorrows, worries, and wisdom regarding the issues plaguing our current and future generations.

We live in a world of challenges that were unheard of just a few decades or years ago—the reign of the Internet, nontraditional family structures, and increasingly fractured relationships, for example. And yet, a grandmother's wisdom will never go out of fashion. Grandmothers, with their lifetime of experience, have more knowledge than anyone since Solomon. Simply put, Nana has a hotline to God! How can she fulfill her role as a godly grandma in the face of modern-day issues?

Based on the sharing from the grandmothers on NanaHood's Facebook page, *The Faith-Filled Grandmother* will discuss the most common and relevant problems at length—from grandmothers who raise grandchildren themselves to long-distance grandmothers; from grandmothers who spoil their grandkids to those who wish to keep them spiritually focused in a material world. Each chapter is followed by God's promise, an appropriate prayer, and practical advice from grandmothers who share personal stories about how they overcame.

This is a prayerful guidebook and spiritual resource for the modern-day Nana. Whether you're a veteran grandma who shares these same challenges or you're a first-time Nana, the promises in these chapters will offer encouragement to every reader who hopes to sustain godly traditions in the family and leave a lasting spiritual legacy.

CHAPTER 1

Grandparent Building Blocks

I'll be honest. When my son said, "You are going to be a grandmother," I thought he was talking to someone standing behind me. After all, I wasn't old enough, was I? I ran to the mirror and peered closely at my reflection. In my mind grandmothers were supposed to look like Grandma Layne, my maternal grandmother. She was large, soft, and cuddly in all the right places, with gray hair and black-rimmed glasses. The woman looking back at me from the mirror was built like Popeye's wife, Olive Oil, and she was about as cuddly as a bean pole.

Not only did I not look like Grandma Layne, I didn't act like her either. She was a homemaker who made biscuits and gravy from scratch every day. She had the patience of Mother Teresa. She never complained about anything and always had time to play games or read books with each one of her grandchildren. My biscuits are Pillsbury, and I can't sit still long enough to play games.

What kind of grandma serves her grandchildren biscuits from a bag and refuses to play Candy Land? The answer to that question is obviously, *I am*, and maybe you are as well.

Grandmothers of the Past

My grandmother was born in 1913, and she and my grandfather married during the Great Depression. Their income (what little there was) came from farming. The cash crop in southern Kentucky where they lived was tobacco, and every family that could raise it did so because it paid the taxes and gave them a little something to put toward seed and plants in the spring.

Tobacco didn't provide enough money for groceries or any extras, so they raised all their food and had milk cows and a few hogs. In addition to gardening, canning, washing, sewing, and cooking on a wood stove, my grandmother also cared for her invalid mother-in-law and her three children. My mother was the middle child, and she and her brothers worked from the time they were old enough to toddle until they left home. By the time the grandchildren arrived, my grandfather was in poor health. My grandparents got by on Social Security. I'm sure my parents helped them out financially, though it was never mentioned. After my grandfather died, it wasn't until my grandmother was in her eighties and I started to help care for her that I found out her total monthly income was around $250.

Why does my grandmother's background matter? The same reason your family history matters. We learn how to be mothers and grandmothers from those who raise us. In some cases, maybe we learn from a neighbor, a friend, or a member of our church family; but what we experience as a child goes with us for the rest of our lives.

Today's Grandmothers and Choices

If I had to mention just one thing that made the biggest difference between the life I lead and the life my grandmother led, it would be without a doubt the amount of choices I have that weren't available to her. Perhaps your grandmother, too, was a member of my Grandma Layne's generation. Think about the opportunities we have today that our grand-mothers didn't.

My grandmother would have never dreamed of going to college. I, on the other hand, never considered that I wouldn't get a degree. Most women my age have had careers. Many of us are still working, some because of necessity and some just because we enjoy what we do. Grandmothers today may choose to grow their own food and can or freeze it, but they also have the option of shopping at supermarkets where the selection of food items would seem mind-boggling to past generations.

Another big difference between grandmothers then and now is how we spend our leisure time. My grandmother darned socks or knitted in her spare time. Eventually, she and my grandfather were able to afford a telephone and a television with an antenna that got three stations, sometimes just two if the wind wasn't blowing from the right direction. They didn't go to sporting events or movies because they didn't have the money. They got up when the sun rose and worked until the sun set in the evening.

When you think about a typical day in the life of my grandmother and compare it to a typical day in mine, it's obvious that times have changed. I talk to more people in a single day than my grandmother probably did in a year. Her world was very limited.

With the invention of the Internet, our world is global.

Is it any wonder that many of us struggle to balance our home and work lives?

Life Is Full of Surprises

The mom I thought I would be evolved into one who had to cope with a lot of problems she wasn't expecting. The grandmother I hoped to be is doing the same.

Grandmothers don't have to look like Betty White, be as much fun as Mary Poppins, craft like Martha Stewart, or bake like Julia Child for our grandchildren to love us. Throw all your inadequacies out the car window and roll it back up.

Everyone has the potential to be a wonderful grandmother—*everyone*, no exceptions. I know now that just as there are no perfect mothers, there are also no perfect grandmothers. The key to being a good grandmother is to use your own personal strengths and talents to connect with your grandchildren. Once the connection is made, opportunities will present themselves for you to share your love.

The Best Book Available for Grandparents

There are many self-help books that provide grandparents with helpful advice. But the best place to look for guidance as a parent or a grandmother is in the Bible.

There are two kinds of legacies we can pass down to those we leave behind—monetary and spiritual. In the Bible, Timothy's grandmother, Lois, raised her daughter, Eunice, to have the same "sincere faith" she had, and because of that Timothy grew up to be rooted in the word. I don't know about you, but I had much rather leave my children and grandchildren a spiritual legacy, like Lois did, than a monetary one. Money won't last, but Heaven is eternal.

> "But from everlasting to everlasting the
> LORD's love is with those who fear him,
> and his righteousness with their children's
> children." (Psalm 103:17)[1]

Grandmothers and mothers have such an important job when it comes to their children and grandchildren. What they see us do and hear us say will echo in their hearts for the rest of their lives. We may not realize it now, but we are creating impressions on young minds that may influence where our grandchildren spend eternity.

---

1 Unless otherwise noted, all scripture references are taken from the New International Version, 2011.

Fruits of the Spirit for Grandmothers

One way we can be a better grandmother is by cultivating the fruits of the Spirit in our lives.

"But the fruit of the Spirit is love, joy, peace, forbearance, kindness, goodness, faithfulness, gentleness and self-control." (Galatians 5:22–23)

Let's take them one at a time and see how they can help us leave a stronger spiritual legacy for our grandchildren.

Love

We love our grandchildren, but do we love them the way the Bible instructs us to love them?

My mother's favorite chapter in the Bible was 1 Corinthians 13, and I'm sure many grandmothers are familiar with it. Reflect on these verses for just a moment.

"Love is patient, love is kind. It does not envy, it does not boast, it is not proud. It does not dishonor others, it is not self-seeking, it is not easily angered, it keeps no record of wrongs. Love does not delight in evil but rejoices with the truth. It always

protects, always trusts, always hopes,
always perseveres."
(1 Corinthians 13:4–7)

If we love our grandchildren the way Christ loved us, we will let our light shine in their lives and be aware and sensitive to their spiritual well-being. We will pray about them and with them when the opportunity presents itself and invite them to attend church with us—whether with their parents or without them if the parents don't attend.

Joy

Do you know the song little children sing in Sunday School about having "joy, joy, joy, joy down in their hearts"?

Children consider joy to mean happiness, but it is really much more than just a euphoric feeling when something good happens. True joy comes from knowing Jesus and having Him planted deep in our hearts. We can have joy even during difficult times by depending on the Lord. James says in James 1:2–3: "Consider it pure joy, my brothers and sisters, whenever you face trials of many kinds, because you know that the testing of your faith produces perseverance."

We don't get to be old enough to be a grandmother

without experiencing trials of many kinds—but if we remember to count it as joy, we will persevere!

Peace

My cousin and best friend, Martha, fought breast cancer for decades. She went through numerous rounds of chemotherapy, lost her hair, and eventually lost her life. But she never lost her faith in God or her sense of peace. One of her favorite passages was Philippians 4:6–7: "Do not be anxious about anything, but in every situation, by prayer and petition, with thanksgiving, present your requests to God. And the peace of God, which transcends all understanding, will guard your hearts and your minds in Christ Jesus."

She was an inspiration not just to me, but to all who knew and loved her. Near the end of her life, I would drive her to her brain radiation treatments. One day, I handed her my cell phone and asked her to make a video while I drove. I interviewed her on our way to the cancer center and then uploaded it to my channel on YouTube (https://t.co/fA3bt-JboMG). Any time I need a reminder of how to find peace in the midst of turmoil, I watch her video. One of the last things she says in the recording is, "Every day may not be good, but there is good in every day."

What a spiritual legacy she left for her children and grandchildren!

Patience

Grandma Layne was the most patient person I have ever known. My grandfather (her husband), on the other hand, was very nervous. The little white farmhouse they lived in had a screen door that led from the kitchen to the porch. I couldn't count all the times he admonished us to not slam the screen door. I'm sure we made him jump every time we forgot and it slammed. But when it came to my grandmother, instead of yelling at us like my grandfather did, she would pull us aside and quietly explain why we shouldn't run in and out of the house and bang the door. Her calm voice and quiet admonishment made a lasting impression on all her grandchildren.

I don't know if patience came easily to her or if she had to work at it. All I know is she had an abundant supply.

What a blessing we are to those around us when we exhibit patience!

Kindness

I don't remember much about my other paternal grandmother, Grandma Bell, as I was only eighteen months old when she died. What I do know about her I learned from others. My mother told me often that one of Grandma Bell's favorite sayings was, "It doesn't cost anything to be kind." And it doesn't.

If our grandchildren see us treating others with kindness, it will make an impression on them. Some of the best examples of kindness I've ever seen have been exhibited by little children. In a world that is often cold and cruel, kindness matters.

"Be kind and compassionate to one another, forgiving each other, just as in Christ God forgave you." (Ephesians 4:32)

Goodness

"Let us not become weary in doing good, for at the proper time we will reap a harvest if we do not give up." (Galatians 6:9)

I have an aunt who is seventy-three years old and who shows no signs of slowing down. She golfs every day, attends exercise classes, and plays tennis. She can still fit into her high school prom dress!

I'm sure she gets tired; but if she does, she doesn't show it. I did not inherit her energy level and I do get weary a lot more easily these days than I once did. But when it comes to doing good, I have to keep moving forward. Doing good does more than saying what we believe. It is faith in action.

Doing good doesn't have an age limit. There is no retirement plan for Christians in this life, but we have Heaven waiting for us on the other side!

Faithfulness

Faith is a fruit that comes with time, prayer, and study. It starts out as a seed and grows into a beautiful, fully bloomed flower.

When you meet someone with great faith, you can see it, feel it, and hear it in their speech. My mother and grandmother were both great women of faith. When my mother was diagnosed with terminal colon cancer at the age of fifty and told she had approximately one year left to live, her faith became more evident to all who knew her. As a mother, she was my friend and teacher her whole life—but during that last year especially she taught me so much about faith.

This life isn't always easy, and neither is being a grandmother. My friend, Jessica, hasn't seen her granddaughter in over a year due to a family disagreement with her son and his wife. Every holiday, every birthday, every day, is a challenge to her faith.

She continues in prayer and walks in faith that one day they can resolve their differences and she will see her granddaughter again. But it's hard. Paul reminds us to "live by faith, not by sight" (2 Corinthians 5:7). If we want stronger faith, then we have to exercise our faith muscles: with prayer and study.

It also helps to be with others who have strong faith because their influence strengthens us. Anyone who has ever been around a negative person (even if they claim to have faith) knows they drag you down. To grow your faith, associate with others who are positive and confidant in their faith.

> "Therefore encourage one another and build each other up, just as in fact you are doing."
> (1 Thessalonians 5:11)

Gentleness

Gentleness goes hand in hand with kindness. Grandma Layne was as gentle as she was kind. She was never loud or rude. She didn't lose her temper and had the softest touch and humblest manner I've ever known.

> "Blessed are the meek, for they will inherit the earth." (Matthew 5:5)

Being humble and meek are fruits that are to be desired. Society disagrees and encourages a "Look at me, I'm great" attitude, but that's not what the Bible says. I don't know about you, but I'd rather put my faith in God than in society any day!

Self-Control

Men and women have struggled with self-control since the beginning of time. Just look at Adam and Eve. They had it all but couldn't control the desire to eat from the one tree God told them not to touch.

Jesus knew that we have fleshly desires that demand self-control. Remember when he was in the garden and he asked the disciples to pray for him? They tried but soon fell asleep. He said, "Watch and pray so that you will not fall into temptation. The spirit is willing, but the flesh is weak" (Matthew 26:41).

We are weak and this fruit of the spirit is challenging. But if we work hard on the other fruit, we can achieve a high level of self-control. Will we ever be able to control our desires all the time? Probably not. We stumble, we fall—but we keep trying. Just like the disciples in the garden who fell asleep when Jesus asked them to stay awake, we will fail sometimes, but He understands and forgives.

Our grandchildren will fail to have self-control too, especially if they are younger. As we grow up, it gets easier to control ourselves when it comes to sin. By the time you are a grandmother you'll have had a lot of experience in coping with self-control. So, we have to be patient with our grandchildren as they struggle with the challenges presented to them by today's fast-paced world.

God's Promises

God has a lot to say about perfection. He knows we cannot go without sinning and that we aren't perfect.

Remember when Paul had a physical problem (he referred to it as his thorn) and he prayed for it to be removed?

"And He has said to me, 'My grace is sufficient for you, for power is perfected in weakness.' Most gladly, therefore, I will rather boast about my weaknesses, so that the power of Christ may dwell in me." (2 Corinthians 12:9, NASB)

(continued)

Our weakness is where God can do the most. Examine your weaknesses and pray about them.

Instead of seeking to be the perfect grand-mother, seek the will of God, and in doing so you will become a better (not perfect) grandmother!

A Grandmother's Prayer

Dear Lord, help us to remember that there are no perfect grandmothers. But through Bible study and prayer, you can mold us into the grandmothers you want us to be. Help us plant the seed of God's word deep inside our grandchildren's hearts so that they will grow up to be servants in your kingdom. Amen.

Advice from Grandmothers

"Unconditional love . . . no matter what. Even if they desert you or grow up and have their own lives, you love them every day, think of them every day, miss them every day. No matter how many times you see them you hug them like they have been away forever, and when they leave hug them like you will never see them again. . . . Oh, and ice cream and cookies don't hurt. :)" —Jeanie J.

"There isn't one [perfect grandma]. But I can promise all the grandmothers out there that they are a vision of perfection in the eyes of their grandchild. She's the one who caves at a smile, the first step, or the first time hearing *Nana* or *Grammy*. She will proudly pick you up from school and daycare, take you to playdates and doctor appointments, and do whatever it takes to help Mom and Dad raise a happy, well-balanced child in today's world. But most of all she is the cookie baker, craft teacher,

(continued)

17

running-through-the-sprinkler dancer, and lap-hugging, face-kissing, bear-hugging, bubble-blowing happiest person on earth because she's a Grandmother." —Leona C.

"Someone who is always there. A second chance at parenthood. Unconditional love. Butterflies in the pit of your stomach when you know you are going to spend time with your grandchild, and an ache in your heart when it's time for them to leave. Loving every precious moment." —Wendy

"The perfect grandparents for most children (I hope) are the ones they have. Sadly, we know this isn't always the case. But for most kids, these are the ones who show up for birthday parties and family dinners, always slipping a little cash in their pockets or taking them out for ice cream, always willing to listen, always interested, always just letting them be who they are, and always, always, always having their back—those are the "perfect" grandparents." —Jimmie A.

"I'm answering as a special needs grandparent. I think you need to be someone who is present and supportive, willing to learn how to care for your grandchildren and be there for the parents." —Kelley

"I don't think there IS a "perfect grandmother," but a good grandma gives her grandchildren her time and energy, creates memories, and gives herself freely and unconditionally. She is the confidant of their dreams and wishes (and sometimes the maker of some of them). She is forever there to greet them with a smile, open arms, and a full heart. She always provides a safe haven for them!" —Jill

"A grandparent is someone who loves unconditionally. Is always there to talk, play, advise, bake cookies, cry with them, snuggle, and give unlimited hugs and kisses. Grandparents can help their grandchild have fond memories of growing up. They make you feel special." —Christi

"Cool and groovy, supplying unconditional love and lots of attention equally to all her grandkids." —Hayley

"Supportive and nonjudgmental. All kids need

(continued)

19

a safe adult to talk to and to also vent their frustrations with." —Pamela

"There is no such thing as the 'perfect grandmother.' We love with all we have inside us. We give them all our wisdom of life." —Kimmie

CHAPTER 2

The Long-Distance Grandparent

Both sets of my grandparents were farmers who lived in the same small, rural community where I grew up. Most of my friends grew up with grandparents who lived nearby or at least close enough that they could see them within a couple of hours of travel.

But things have changed. Today, grandparents often live in different cities, states, and sometimes different countries than their grandchildren.

Sometimes, if grandparents are located far away from their grandchildren, they may decide to move closer to be near them. One grandmother I know has moved three different times to three different states to be near her son and grandchildren. Another grandfather I know moved to be near his son and their grandchildren. After one year, the grandfather had already taken a job and settled in for what he thought would be a long-term arrangement—until he found out that his son was being transferred again. "My advice to other grandparents is to make sure they like where they are moving to because they may get left behind," he said.

The good news is that you don't have to spend a lot of time with your grandchildren to create strong bonds. While being a hands-on grandparent is preferable, virtual grandmothers can bond with their grandchildren as well.

For grandparents who want to be involved with their grandchildren but are separated by distance, there is probably no better time to be alive. With the advancements in technology, there are ways grandparents can see and interact with their grandchildren that our grandparents would have never imagined possible. No longer are we limited to expensive phone calls. With FaceTime and Skype, we can see their faces and hear those precious voices no matter how far away we are!

If you are about to be a first-time grandparent or you already have grandchildren but haven't stirred up the courage to try new ways of communication, don't be afraid to ask for help. Ask a friend or neighbor to help you get started and teach you to use your computer to connect with your loved ones. You can also go to your local library. Even if you don't have an expensive phone or the Internet in your home, there are still places where you can go online and visit with loved ones. Don't let another day go by without investigating how you can use technology to spend time communicating with your grandchildren.

It is especially important that you build a strong bond with them during the first five years of life. These are known as the formative years, and it is during this time that a young child's brain is developing and getting ready to learn the social skills they'll need early on. You don't want to miss any of their precious milestones, and you don't have to—if you are willing to let technology help you!

One at a Time

There is a lot of research out there about being a grandparent. One thing all the studies I've read agree on is that it's best to bond with one grandchild at a time. If you are trying to FaceTime with multiple grandchildren at once it's going to be chaotic at best, but if each child has ten minutes of their own, not only is it easier to converse with them, but also they will share things they couldn't have shared if they were competing for your time and attention.

The same thing happens when grandparents come for a visit, or vice versa. If each child gets special alone time with the grandparent, it's easier to talk and you can make the most of your one-on-one time. Perhaps each child could choose a favorite park to go to, or restaurant you can take them to. Anything to spend quality time with each individual grandchild.

Most of the grandparents I know love to read stories to their grandchildren—and you can still read to your grands even if they live far away. Buy two copies of a favorite book and mail one copy to them so you can read together. They will love hearing you read to them.

A friend of mine actually babysits her grandchildren via Skype. Here is how it works. Her grandchild is eighteen months old. Her mom places her in the playpen with a few toys (nothing she could choke on) and then arranges the computer on a table close enough for the grandchild to see her grandmother, but far away enough that she can't reach it. Then Mom cleans, does laundry, or takes a quick shower. She is close by but is able to do a few chores while Grandma entertains! In case of an emergency, Grandma and Mom have cell phones with them, should either one of them have to cut the visit short.

If your grandchildren are preteens or teens, there is a good chance they are texting. If you don't know how to text, learn. You may not like communicating that way, but they do and it's a great way to stay in touch. Sometimes it's much easier to talk to Grandma about a problem than Mom, and even easier if you don't have to look them in the eyes. Texting provides that mode of communication.

Parents have the hard job of setting boundaries, completing a zillion daily chores, and making discipline decisions. Grandparents are cheerleaders, mentors, and self-esteem builders. How blessed it is to be a grandparent!

One day, when I was eating lunch at a restaurant, I overheard the lady at the next table say, "I raised my kids; why would I want to be involved with my grandchildren? They live down the street, but I usually just see them at Thanksgiving and Christmas. That's enough time for me." I almost fell out of my chair. It never occurred to me that there were grandmothers who felt like that! What joy they are missing! I felt sad for her and wondered if she knew how many grandmothers would love to trade places with her, especially those who live far away from their grands.

There are some things we can change and other things we can't. If our children move far away, we have the option of moving closer or visiting when time and circumstances allow. If we can't, the option of technology allows us to remain connected no matter how far the physical distance is between us.

Perhaps one of the best-known prayers is the Serenity Prayer. Written by American theologian Reinhold Niebuhr, it goes like this, "God, grant me the serenity to accept the things I cannot change, courage to change the things I can, and wisdom to know the difference."

It's a great prayer for parents and grandparents to remember.

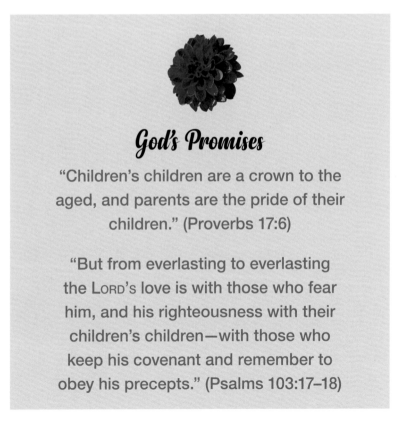

God's Promises

"Children's children are a crown to the aged, and parents are the pride of their children." (Proverbs 17:6)

"But from everlasting to everlasting the LORD's love is with those who fear him, and his righteousness with their children's children—with those who keep his covenant and remember to obey his precepts." (Psalms 103:17–18)

A Grandmother's Prayer

Dear Lord, our children's children are precious to us and we want so very much to be a positive influence on their lives. When there is distance between us, help us find ways to connect with them so that they may know our love is like your love—it knows no boundaries. They are connected to our hearts, and we love them so very much. I will pray for them daily and let them know they are loved as often as I possibly can. Amen.

Advice from Grandmothers

While no one would ever suggest that technology can substitute for actually being with your grandchildren in person, as you can see by these grandmother's statements, there are many ways to spend time together even when you are far apart.

"We moved away from our granddaughter when she was six years old. I asked her to be my pen pal. She is now almost thirteen and we have kept up the lost art of writing letters to one another all these years! It has kept us in touch and made her a good writer. She has learned cursive and also uses a typewriter at times. I believe this has had a positive influence. I also convey many thoughts and much advice, especially now that she is maturing. We talk on the phone and FaceTime, too, but we still continue our letter writing. I'm saving her letters and I hope she is saving mine." —**Marylys**

"My granddaughter told me she liked it when her other grandmother would color half of a coloring book page, mail it to her to finish, and then she would mail it back. This allowed her to get mail, which she loved. We made some great memories this way." —Linda

"I use a texting app (WhatsApp) with my grandchildren as they all live far away. My youngest grandchild is three. He doesn't always chat but when he does he shows me lots of things and at least knows me by sight. That way, when we do see each other I'm not a stranger." —Karen

"My two great-grandchildren lived with us for two years while my granddaughter was deployed. She is home now and they moved away last month. They video chatted with their mother, and now they do it with me. They are five and eight now, so holding their attention is sometimes hard, but I cherish each visit." —Judi

"When I lived a distance from my grandson, we loved FaceTime. Even if it was thirty minutes

(continued)

of him making faces and showing me things in his room. One time he propped the phone up so I could watch him play." —Sharlene

"A nana I knew whose granddaughter lived abroad used to read to her over FaceTime. Both of them really enjoyed it, and it gave her granddaughter a love of reading." —Shelia

"A friend bakes with her grandchildren via FaceTime. They choose the recipe and the daughter sends her a copy. They assemble the ingredients and Nana cooks on one coast while her grandchildren make the same recipe on the other side of the country. They all have fun and end up with treats to eat." —Sue

"We found a book that allows you to record your voice telling the story. Our twin grandsons loved it so much they eventually wore it out." —Rosemarie

"I bought my granddaughter a cloud pet and we send messages through it. (Cloud pets are stuffed animals that can send and receive messages via the iCloud.)" —Donna

CHAPTER 3

The Grandmother Who Spoils

To spoil, or not to spoil? Is there anything wrong with being the grandmother who gives her grandchild lots of sweets and gifts? That depends on who you ask.

If my mother were still alive today and you asked her about spoiling her grandchildren, she would assure you that it was her right to do so and that she loved doing it. She always brought them "surprises" when she traveled, and when it was their birthday or Christmas she made sure they had enough presents to make an impressive stack of gifts. Truthfully, she gave them too much, but it brought her such joy that I couldn't say no. And then when my children were three, five, and seven years old, she died from colon cancer. I was so thankful that I had never mentioned how much she spoiled them. It was one of her ways of showing them love. She was giving her grandchildren all the things she had missed out on as a child. Mom was raised on a small farm in rural Kentucky. Her first dresses were made from feed sacks. Holidays and birthdays might bring gifts of fruit, usually an orange or tangerine and some peppermints. That was it. By the time my brother and I came along, she was able to give us things she had yearned for but couldn't afford.

In contrast to my mother, her mother (my maternal grandmother) simply couldn't afford monetary gifts. But still I always felt her love. My grandmother gave me the gift of her time and patience. She spent hours with all her grandchildren and read to us from a collection of little books she had on a bookcase that she kept behind her rocking chair. None of her grandchildren ever felt neglected or left out. She shared whatever she had, and that was more than enough.

Did my mother love her grandchildren more than my grandmother loved hers? Of course not. They both loved their grandchildren in their own ways and shared what they had. My mother was able to give her grandchildren more material things, but if you ask my children what they remember most about her, they'll recall as much of what she did with them as what she gave them. While she might have been a champion at spoiling, she also devoted a lot of time and attention to her grandchildren. My mother loved going to the hair salon and getting her hair and nails done. She took my daughter with her and let her get a manicure each time. It's one of my daughter's favorite childhood memories. And because mom loved books so much, she bought and read them enough books to fill a small library.

My cousin Martha loved her grands dearly. I would often visit her during her cancer treatments, and if we went shopping she was always on the lookout for something her grandchildren might like. On one occasion, she had several items piled up high on the counter. As the lady rang them up, I jokingly said, "You realize you are spoiling your grandchildren rotten."

She looked at me and smiled. "And I plan to continue for just as long as the good Lord will let me."

Martha died three years ago, and her family will always miss her giving spirit. The material things she left them don't matter, but her love of giving just to bring them joy will be a memory they will cherish forever.

Because Martha had grandchildren who lived in two different states, one set near her and the other far away, she was careful to spoil them evenly. If she bought for one set at one store, then she was certain to shop for the others at the next store. She never showed favoritism.

Remember the story of Jacob and Esau. Their parents Rebecca and Isaac made the mistake of choosing favorites, which had a disastrous outcome. When it comes to spoiling, whatever your opinion is, treat every grandchild the same or be ready to deal with the consequences.

When I surveyed grandmothers to find out how they felt about spoiling, I received a wide variety of answers. One grandmother, Jackie, wrote to me and said, "I have been raising my grandchildren since birth so I must treat them like I did my own. I worry more about teaching them respect and obedience."

Each and every grandparent is different and has their own unique perspective about spoiling. Instead of judging one another or criticizing, why not listen to their thoughts and opinions and realize that the most important gift we can give them is love—and how we show *that* depends on many different things: our background, the time we get to spend with them, and our relationship with their parents.

Speaking of Parents

We have to obey the ground rules set by our children (our grandchildren's parents). If they don't want us giving gifts or treats, then we don't need to go against their wishes. A long conversation about what is okay and what isn't when it comes to spoiling can go a long way toward keeping the peace.

One thing that grandparents who are big gift givers need to remember is you can't buy love. By constantly bringing them material gifts, you're teaching them that "stuff matters." Instead of giving them things, why not give them memories by doing fun activities together? Instead of a new doll (my granddaughter has so many they won't all fit in a toy box), take them with you to shop for Christmas toys for underprivileged children during the holidays. Let them help wrap and deliver the gifts. I promise it's something they will never forget. I know because my mother did this, and I vividly remember the feeling of joy it created in me as I gave to others.

Description of a Grandmother

One way you can determine if you are spoiling your grandchildren too much is to ask them to describe you. Depending on how old your grandchildren are, you will get a variety of answers—but if they talk about the things you give them rather than the things you do with them, you may be giving them more material gifts than memories. In Charles Swindell's wonderful book *The Tale of the Tardy Oxcart*, there is an essay by an unknown author that speaks to the importance of the grandmother-grandchild relationship.

What Is a Grandmother?
By a Third Grader

A grandmother is a lady who has no children of her own. She likes other people's little boys and girls. A grandfather is a man grandmother. He goes for walks with the boys, and they talk about fishing, football, and stuff like that. Grandmothers don't have anything to do except to be there. They're old so they shouldn't play hard or run. It is enough if they drive us to the store where the pretend horse is, and have lots of change ready. Or, if they take us for walks, they slow down past things like pretty leaves and caterpillars. They never say "hurry up."

Usually grandmothers are fat, but not too

fat to tie your shoes. They wear glasses and funny underwear. They can take their teeth and gums off.

Grandmothers don't have to be smart, only answer questions like, "Why isn't God married?" and "How come dogs chase cats?"

Grandmothers don't talk baby talk like other visitors do, because it's hard to understand. When they read to us, they don't skip or mind if it's the same story over again.

Everybody should try to have a grandmother, especially if you're not allowed to watch much television, because they are the only grown-ups who have time.

I suspect that most grandchildren, even those older than this third grader, need more "time spoiling" than "gift spoiling," don't you?

God's Promises

As a grandmother of faith, I take all God's promises seriously.

> "Seek ye first the kingdom of God,
> and his righteousness; and all these
> things shall be added unto you."
> (Matthew 6:33, KJV)

This verse also applies to the relationships with our grandchildren. If we love them and want to help them grow strong spiritually, we must keep them focused on the kingdom of Heaven. With that in mind, I believe that gifts of our time, our thoughts, and our wisdom are the gifts that benefit our grandchildren the most. Spoiling them with material gifts occasionally is fun—but the greater blessing is the gift of your time and attention.

A Grandmother's Prayer

Dear Lord, we love our grandchildren so much and we want to give them gifts to bring them joy. But please help us remember that true joy, happiness, and peace comes from a relationship with you. If we want them to have the blessings that come from following in your footsteps, we have to spend time with them, teach them, and talk with them about you and your word. And then we have to show them how to live what we teach them. Amen.

Advice from Grandmothers

"We indulge our grandchildren in many different ways; our time, activities, special food, and gifts. Their parents are number one and we follow their wishes as best we can. They are good parents and if we ever have any doubts about their ability to do right by their children, we would discuss the problem with them and help them in any way we could." —Christine

"My one and only grand, age three, is the light of my life, and I SHOW it! He has always felt it. Just love. Nothing else. I think his parents are doing a great job, loving and not spoiling. I admire how they raise him." —Carolyn

"I do spoil mine . . . but I expect them to be respectful and do as they are told. They have manners and they behave in public." —Cindy

"I love my granddaughter, but I also love her parents. I remember how frustrated I used to get when our rules for children weren't

followed. If our granddaughter's parents tell us their rules or guidelines for her, I follow them. They are great parents, and I want her to grow up with their values. Spoiling her won't help her grow up to be a strong young woman."
—Susan

"I think spoiling your grandchildren is okay to a point. Time and hugs are most important and small gifts are fine. However, it's not okay to play favorites between grandchildren. Be fair, loving, and kind. Help your children raise respectful, responsible, kind, caring adults."
—Carla

"I love having the time and resources to spoil my grandson, which I didn't have when raising my own two children. But I'm also aware that part of my role is to support my daughter and son-in-law. I want to help them raise a happy, respectful child." —Kathleen

"I spoil mine, but to a degree. I still believe in reprimanding them and letting them know that their parents have the final say."
—Gina

(continued)

"We can spoil our grandchildren, but we don't go against the parents' wishes because it causes arguments." —**Sue**

"Spoiling is the grandparents' job!" —**Debby**

"I have four grandsons—one who lives with me, one in Texas, and two who are about three miles from me! I truly believe that you should respect the parents' wishes and abide by the rules they have made. It shows respect for them as parents! I go all out during their birthdays (with the approval of the parents) and I treat them the same. This is important in raising them to be amazing men!" —**Clarise**

"We can spoil them with love, time, and fun. I don't spoil mine with material things. They don't really care about those things. I try to help my daughter by sticking to her rules when they are with me." —**Lorraine**

"I spoil them a bit more than my children, but I still have ground rules." —**Sheila**

"I feel we should be the ones to give special treats and if we are able to get the awesome gift. But that's the perk of being Nanny.

Spoiling them outright doesn't help them become responsible little humans." —**Mona**

"There is nothing wrong with spoiling a grandchild to a point, especially with love. However, everything has a limit. No child should get everything they want. You also have to respect the parents' wishes. If Mom and Dad say no to certain foods, for example, then don't be the grandparent that gives it to them anyway." —**Sheila**

CHAPTER 4

Keeping Children Spiritually Focused in a Material World

There are so many distractions for children in the course of a day. Keeping them spiritually focused seems like an impossible task, but it isn't. There are many ways that grandparents can help their grandchildren develop a strong spiritual foundation. One of the reasons I'm so sure about this is because my grandmother influenced me so profoundly that I can only hope to have half the impact on my grandchildren that she did on me.

How did she do it? By the way she lived. Her life was her biggest and most important sermon.

If we want to help our children who are parents to create their own spiritually minded children, we have to do as my grandmother did—model Christian behavior. We can be engaged in our church community, pray with our grandchildren, and when possible bring them to Sunday worship and church activities. We can't just tell them that they need to be spiritually focused; we have to show them what that means.

A few weeks ago I took three of my grandchildren to an all-day event sponsored by a lady at our church. They loved doing crafts, exploring nature, and spending a day with Nana just having fun!

If you are wondering how you can be influential if you live far away, just remember: where there is a will, there is a way! Use FaceTime or Skype to share thoughts and conversations. Read children's Bible stories to them online. Watch a video of a Bible story online and discuss it together. Mail them books that have spiritual themes and a copy of a children's Bible. Write them letters and share stories about what God has done in your life. Be present as much as possible, either by visiting them or using technology, and encourage them by listening to their bedtime prayers or discussing what they are thankful for. If possible, invite them to spend part of their summer vacation with you or plan their visits while your Vacation Bible School is going on.

But it's important to remember that parents are the primary caretakers of their children. You never want to do anything that goes against their wishes, even if it's something you feel strongly about.

Once, I spoke at a conference for grandparents and noticed that a gentleman in the front row was crying. When I got to the question-and-answer section of the program, I knew he had something he wanted to say. "My children will not let me talk about my faith to my grandchildren," he said tearfully. "If I do they have assured me I will never see them again."

I did my best to reassure him that the life he lived would compensate for not being able to talk to his grandchildren specifically about faith. I told him about the lessons I'd learned from my grandmother. I hope and pray that he was somewhat comforted by my words.

Grandparents and parents cannot force faith on a child. We merely plant the seeds and then water them with prayer and trust God to help them grow.

Other Things Faith-Filled Grandmothers Can Do

What is faith?

> "Now faith is being sure of what we hope
> for and certain of what we do not see. This
> is what the ancients were commended for."
> (Hebrews 11:1–2, NIV 1984)

A faith-filled grandmother is *sure* and *certain* of things she doesn't see. The beginning of faith is belief in God and knowing that he is who he says he is. The ending point is believing in God's promises. God has done what he said he would and will continue to do what he has promised to do.

If you are a faith-filled grandmother, you are extremely important to your family. But sadly, not every Christian grandmother feels important. In many cultures around the world, the older you are, the more you are valued; but in America, emphasis is placed on youth and beauty, which every grandparent knows only lasts for a short time.

Don't believe what society thinks and says about older people. Instead, think about what the Bible says about the power and influence of older Christians. Those we refer to as Faith Heroes in Hebrews

11 had some age on them. And remember: you don't have to be perfect to be a faith-filled grandmother.

One of the heroes in Hebrews 11 was a Gentile and a prostitute. Her name was Rahab, a citizen of the city Jericho. The Hebrews were about to attack Jericho and Joshua, who was in charge at the time, sent spies to gauge how difficult it would be to take the city. Rahab hid the spies and helped them escape, but she was wise enough to make a deal with them before they left—she wanted her family's safety guaranteed. Because of her bravery (if she'd been caught hiding spies, she and her family would have been killed), Joshua honored her request. When the Hebrews attacked, everyone was killed but Rahab and her family. She showed her faith by trusting God to spare her and her family when the city was destroyed. Faith can turn our lives around and cause us to do what is right, regardless of our past.

If you lived close to your grandparents when you were growing up, perhaps you had a grandparent who influenced you. Think about *how* they influenced you. Did they encourage you to go to church? Did they pray with you? Did they talk to you about the beauty of nature and all the wonders of the world that God created? When you ask the children in your family (the ones who are old enough to understand) who influences them the most, usually their first answer is their parents; the second is their grandparents.

When our grandchildren are old enough to understand the concept of faith, one thing we can do is tell them our story of how we came to believe and how God has worked in our lives. There have been so many times in my life when I have looked back at a past event and known with absolute certainty that God caused that something to happen to me for a reason. If you can't tell your grandchildren in person, why not write it down and mail it to them? It's a wonderful way for them to see how God's promises have worked in our lives and how they can in turn work in theirs.

"And we know that in all things God works
for the good of those who love him, who
have been called according to his purpose."
(Romans 8:28)

Study Biblical Women of Faith

If these women lived long enough, they very likely became grandmothers, though their roles as grandmothers are not discussed in the Bible. However, there are things we can learn from each of them that can strengthen our faith.

Mary

Can you imagine how Mary must have felt when Gabriel told her she was going to be the mother of Jesus? She was probably very young, and the news that she would conceive a child of God who would be the Messiah of the world had to shock her to the core.

> "And Mary said, 'Behold, I am the servant of the Lord; let it be to me according to your word.' And the angel departed from her."
> (Luke 1:38, ESV)

Mary was a great example of "trust and obey." I don't imagine her life was an easy one, but every time she is mentioned she is following the will of God. To be faith-filled, we have to be like Mary and have enough faith and trust to obey without hesitation.

Ruth

Ruth loved her mother-in-law, Naomi, so much that she did not want to be separated from her. She followed her to a foreign land full of strangers she did not know. And when her mother-in-law gave her advice, Ruth listened and did what she asked. "'I will do whatever you say,' Ruth answered" (Ruth

3:1–5). As a result of Naomi's guidance, she married Boaz and had a son named Obed. Through her lineage came David and eventually Jesus.

From Ruth we can see the power of the love and respect she had for her mother-in-law. We also see Naomi's faith and wisdom that led her to be a positive influence on Ruth. God took care of them because of their faith, just as he will take care of us.

Esther

Esther led a fascinating, but dangerous, life. As the Jewish wife of a king, she had to make a choice. Should she keep silent about Haman's evil plot to kill the Jews? Or should she speak up and risk her own life? Her decision was a brave one. "Go, gather together all the Jews who are in Susa, and fast for me. Do not eat or drink for three days, night or day. I and my attendants will fast as you do. When this is done, I will go to the king, even though it is against the law. And if I perish, I perish" (Esther 4:16). A faith-filled woman should be courageous like Esther.

Hannah

One of my personal favorite examples of a faith-filled woman was Hannah. One thing I admire about her was she had control of her tongue, something most of us struggle with. Her husband, Elkanah, had another wife, Peninnah, who had children. Hannah was infertile and Peninnah ridiculed and made fun of Hannah. Instead of responding to her, Hannah kept her mouth shut. I can't imagine that was easy to do. Instead, she responded with prayer.

Then, her character was tested when Eli, the prophet, accused her of being drunk. She could have smarted off to him, but once again Hannah demonstrated grace and humility through her words: "Do not regard your servant as a worthless woman, for all along I have been speaking out of my great anxiety and vexation" (1 Samuel 1:16, ESV). Once Hannah explained herself to Eli, he understood. He then told her of God's intention to answer her prayer for a son, and Hannah believed him.

Hannah wasn't the first woman to suffer infertility in the Bible, but she was the first to accept that God would keep his promise without questioning. Sarah laughed when the angel told her that God would give her a child (Genesis 18:12). Rebekah questioned, "If all is well, why am I like this?" as her twins struggled in the womb (Genesis 25:22, NKJV). Rachel gave the responsibility to her husband (Genesis 30:1). But Hannah trusted God without doubt or concern. Her reverent fear of the Lord was just one more quality of her godly character. Eli was right—God answered her prayer.

But the story didn't end when Hannah gave birth to Samuel. When he was still very young, she took him to the temple and gave him up to be a servant to God. I don't know about you, but if I had been infertile for years and suddenly had a son, it would break my heart to give him up. But not Hannah. Just as God kept his promise to her, so she kept her promise to him. And because of what she did each year, Eli blessed her again and again, and she had three more sons and two daughters.

Oh, to be more like Hannah! To be able to speak when appropriate and keep silent when provoked. To have faith that doesn't question and courage to keep her promise to God, even if it meant giving up her son. Hannah was a faith-filled woman, and if she lived long enough to be a grandmother, I just know she was a faith-filled grandmother as well!

God's Promises

These verses show the important role family members play in the raising of kids. Parents and grandparents can follow these instructions to raise godly children and grandchildren.

"You shall teach them diligently to your sons and shall talk of them when you sit in your house and when you walk by the way and when you lie down and when you rise up." (Deuteronomy 6:7, NASB)

"Train up a child in the way he should go: and when he is old, he will not depart from it." (Proverbs 22:6, KJV)

"There was not a word of all that Moses had commanded which Joshua did not read before all the assembly of Israel

(continued)

with the women and the little ones and the strangers who were living among them." (Joshua 8:35, NASB)

"Come, you children, listen to me; I will teach you the fear of the Lord." (Psalm 34:11, NASB)

"My son, do not forget my teaching, But let your heart keep my commandments." (Proverbs 3:1, NASB)

"I have no greater joy than this, to hear of my children walking in the truth." (3 John 1:4, NASB)

A Grandmother's Prayer

Heavenly Father, help me to be a good example to my grandchildren. Help me to teach them by the life that I live and by the words I share. Remind me to let them know I pray for them daily; and when my time on earth is done, may I have lived so that they know I will be in Heaven. Not because of anything I did, but because of what Jesus did for all sinners. Amen.

Advice from Grandmothers

"Take them outside and let God's creation speak to them. Dance in the rain. Show them

(continued)

how every leaf, every flower, every blade of grass is different. Show them an ant colony and explain to them how important their work is . . . each one with a task. Create opportunities that will ignite their souls and speak to their natural curiosity. Plant seeds literally and figuratively and watch them grow." —**Brenda**

"Ask each grandchild what you bought them last year for their birthday or as a Christmas gift. If they do not remember, well, there you go. It is time to step back and take a look at what you are doing. Is it working for their best? What example are you setting for their future habits? Their future children? Get those grandchildren involved with others who don't have. Let them see for themselves just how blessed they are, and how so many others suffer. This works for adults also: leave the world of Me-ism, and take a walk around in someone's life who has been less fortunate. What your eyes will see and your ears will hear will prick your heart, change your focus, and put you in tune with God's unconditional love for his precious babies. The more love we feel, the less self we will see. Go out, let your light shine so others can see." —**Sharon**

"This is something we do each morning with our grandson: we hold hands and say a prayer before he heads out to school. We pray for safety, and for the teachers and the children to have a good day. After we say, 'In Jesus's name, we pray,' he says, 'Amen!'" —**Nancy**

"Sharing with them the simple activities that taught us so much about being content. Making houses out of leaves in the fall, skipping rocks, playing marbles, reading in bed with a flashlight. No electricity needed. That in turn leads to discussions about how God takes care of us and how we need to focus on taking care of other people and their needs. Teaching them the age-old truth: 'No one will care how much you know until they know how much you care.' Grandparents are blessed with so many great opportunities. Sometimes a child will open up to grandparents more than their parent. There's a safety net that equals nothing else." —**Delores**

"My grandchildren take turns spending the night with me. I try to do some spiritual activity with them (prepare communion, visit a

(continued)

friend, make food for someone, etc.). I always make sure we have discussions about vital things." —Debbie

"Turn everyday events into learning experiences. Include them in things that are often thought to be grown up events. About six years ago, I took all three grandchildren and their parents to the Timothy Hill dinner where they learned about its Christ-centered residential programs and retreat centers (www.timothyhill.org). This past summer, they made a trip to New York and worked at the ranch for a few days. I've taken them to Eastern European dinners where they learn about work in Ukraine and the push to get Bibles in all the schools; one grandchild gave all her birthday money for these Bibles. When something bad happens, we talk about it. I want them to know that Satan is not make-believe and that he wants to destroy good. We serve a community meal for the poor each week at church; I have helped cook for this for ten years. Now, I take the grandchildren with me. They help cook and register people as they come in. I tell them Bible stories, and when I'm working on a lesson for the ladies' class, I often tell them what I'm doing. It's a matter of turning off the TV and talking!" —**Deanna**

"I think one of the most helpful things we can do is use God's teachings as we go about life with our grands. When they do something kind, helpful, useful, or show compassion, etc., we can tell them we're proud of them, and that God is proud of them as well. And if we want, we can turn to the scripture to back that up. When they're asking about things that might seem questionable, again, we can bring God's teaching into the conversation. He's real. And I think we need to talk about Him more—about His approval, when we make Him sad, about His forgiveness when we make mistakes. Sometimes it seems we've gotten away from talking about Him as a reality and relegate Him to 'religion' rather than 'life.'" —**Joyce**

"Though my grandchildren currently have everything they could ever want from loving parents and grandparents, I do worry, in their case, that all they have might prevent them from finding a spiritual path in a material

(continued)

world. Their mother is very spiritual. She approaches every day with thankfulness and has passed that to the children. Yes, there will be challenges; that's a given as they grow up. But they live in a household devoted to reading and creating, and I believe that mental involvement will serve them well. Should they hesitate, they have their mother and family to remind them that, in the end, material goods are not what matters. Love and relationships are." —Elizabeth

"I feel strongly about their spiritual development and took them all to Sunday school during the early years. Now as they're older, I show by example, attending church myself each week, bringing God and faith into conversations and situations. I'm not church-lady-like; I'm just me. Kids do grasp so much even when it appears they're not paying attention." —Joan

CHAPTER 5

Grandmothers Who Worry

If my grandmother worried about her children and grandchildren, she never shared any of her concerns with me. My mother, on the other hand, worried about a lot of things. She didn't have to tell me; I saw it on her face. She carried a lot of burdens on her shoulders, and it weighed on her physically and mentally.

If we are faith-filled grandmothers, then isn't it wrong for us to worry? If we believe in God, then why do we find it difficult at times to trust him? Personally, I believe worry is the devil's biggest weapon. He uses it to take away our peace and cause us to forget the awesome power of God. If the devil can get us to worry, then our worry may lead to doubt, and doubt may cause us not to trust.

"Humble yourselves, therefore, under God's mighty hand, that he may lift you up in due time. Cast all your anxiety on him because he cares for you. Be alert and of sober mind. Your enemy the devil prowls around like a roaring lion looking for someone to devour."
(1 Peter 5:6–8)

The Bible tells us over and over not to be afraid—and isn't that what worry is: a fear of something happening to us or a loved one? God wants us to have peace, and there isn't room in our heart for both peace and worry. Consider these two verses about peace.

"Peace I leave with you; my peace I give you. I do not give to you as the world gives. Do not let your hearts be troubled and do not be afraid." (John 14:27)

"Let the peace of Christ rule in your hearts, since as members of one body you were called to peace. And be thankful."
(Colossians 3:15)

My Grandma Layne had hundreds of little wisdom nuggets, timeless quotes passed down from one generation to the next. If I mentioned to her that I was worried about something, she would advise me by saying, "Don't go borrow trouble," which is exactly what we do when we worry!

Jesus said, "Therefore do not worry about tomorrow, for tomorrow will worry about itself. Each day has enough trouble of its own" (Matthew 6:34). That sounds like where Grandma Layne's wisdom nugget originated, doesn't it?

In Their Own Words . . .

In this world, there's no shortage of things to worry about. Just turn on the nightly news, and you are bound to find something to stress over! And not surprisingly, grandmothers tend to worry about the many things connected to their children and grandchildren.

Kathy: "I worry about everything. My granddaughter is in kindergarten and I worry about school shootings and bullying."

Helen: "I worry daily about my grandbabies growing up in a world where no one has respect for anyone else; where people bully and rob, steal and shoot. I am frightened for my babies growing up in this wicked world."

Paula: "I worry about everything. There are so many horrifying things going on in the schools. It was bad enough when my children were growing up. I worry about young kids growing up without having to do chores and handle responsibilities— that they will grow up lazy."

Wanda: "I worry that someone may mistreat my babies. I worry about their future, and I worry about what lies ahead and what they will have to endure. I worry every day, but I also pray every day and thank the good Lord for my many blessings."

Grace: "I worry about the 'middle child' syndrome. Our ten-year-old twin grandson was born first, caught between a smart, athletic big brother and his bossy twin sister. I also worry about my old-est granddaughter's future with Ehlers-Danlos syndrome (an inherited disorder that affects the connective tissues, primarily your skin, joints, and blood vessel walls)."

Gayle: "I worry that their parents will not feel the importance, as I did, to make their children understand what it means to be a leader and not a follower. I was so blessed with the wise choices my children made, and I pray my grandchild will follow in their footsteps."

Kathy: "I worry that I will not be around long enough to see them grow up. That would be so sad. They are the best part of my growing old."

Joy: "I mostly worry that my kids will make the same mistakes in life that I have, thereby adversely affecting my precious grandchildren. I cope with this by encouraging them as they make good parenting decisions, and the positive results are apparent in their families. I refuse to let fear be the ruler."

Nothing New under the Sun

Worry is nothing new. Remember the sisters Mary and Martha in the Bible? Jesus came to visit and while Mary sat and listened to him teach, Martha was distracted by all the housekeeping details. You can almost hear the weariness in Jesus's voice when he says, "Martha, Martha, you are worried and upset about many things, but few things are needed—or indeed only one. Mary has chosen what is better, and it will not be taken away from her" (Luke 10: 41–42).

Essentially, Jesus was chastising Martha for being concerned with something that wasn't really important.

Our children and grandchildren are most certainly important, but worrying about them doesn't do any good. In fact, it can be harmful to our health. Stress and anxiety can lower your immune system, making it easier for you to pick up colds or more serious illnesses. Excessive worry disturbs your peace of mind, which makes it harder for you to concentrate on one task at a time. People who worry a lot often have trouble falling asleep at night, and many of the grandmothers I spoke with said that if they do indeed get to sleep, they wake up frequently and have trouble falling back to sleep.

Stopping Worry

Picture that you are on a train named "Worry" that is leaving the station. It picks up speed and rushes us forward toward our destination.

Now, imagine that you are the conductor of the train and that you are going in the wrong direction. You wanted to go north, but the track you are on is headed south. To get to your destination you have to turn the train around. It won't be easy and it may take some time, but by making some changes in your life and thought patterns, you'll be able to get to where you want to go.

Here are some suggestions to help you turn your "worry train" around:

1. Read and study God's word daily, especially the Bible verses on worry and fear. Set aside a segment of time every day for personal study. Even fifteen minutes is long enough to remind yourself of who you are serving and who is in charge. (Hint: it's not you!) Choose a favorite verse that reminds you not to worry and memorize it. Then next time you start to worry about something, repeat the verse out loud, over and over.

2. Sing a favorite hymn to yourself when you need to relax, or listen to spiritual songs. Music has been used for centuries as a way to calm us when we are anxious. Remember that King Saul called upon David to come play the harp to soothe him and make him feel better.

3. Talk to a friend about whatever is bothering you. "Bear ye one another's burdens, and so fulfill the law of Christ" (Galatians 6:2, KJV). There's nothing

better than having a friend who listens, understands, and prays for you and with you. If you have such a friend, you are blessed. If you don't, consider joining a ladies' Bible study class and cultivating new friends. Chances are whatever you are worrying about can be made less of a burden if you share it with someone else.

4. Increase your prayer time. When my children became teenagers, I spent more time on my knees in prayer than I ever had before. Why? Because I knew my children would be faced with temptations. I knew they would be making choices that could possibly affect the rest of their lives. If you find yourself worrying, pray more. If your mind is occupied with prayer, then it isn't occupied with worry!

5. Something that has personally worked for me when it comes to combatting worry is walking. I actually combine prayer and exercise. I walk up and down my driveway as I talk to God. I praise him for the beauty of my surroundings, my health, and my family and friends. It's a great way to get exercise and one-on-one

time with Jesus. I guess you could call it "prayer-robics"! Not only is prayer-robics good for your health; it also helps you worry less. And you don't have to be a fast walker for this to work; any speed will do as long as you are moving. It's not only the rabbits that win the race . . . turtles who don't give up make it to the finish line, too!

God's Promises

"Come to me, all you who are weary and burdened, and I will give you rest. Take my yoke upon you and learn from me, for I am gentle and humble in heart, and you will find rest for your souls. For my yoke is easy and my burden is light." (Matthew 11:28–30)

(continued)

"Even though I walk through the darkest valley, I will fear no evil, for you are with me; your rod and your staff, they comfort me." (Psalm 23:4)

"Therefore I tell you, do not worry about your life, what you will eat or drink; or about your body, what you will wear. Is not life more than food, and the body more than clothes? Look at the birds of the air; they do not sow or reap or store away in barns, and yet your heavenly Father feeds them. Are you not much more valuable than they? Can any one of you by worrying add a single hour to your life? And why do you worry about clothes? See how the flowers of the field grow. They do not labor or spin. Yet I tell you that not even Solomon in all his splendor was dressed like one of these. If that is how God clothes the grass of the field, which is here today and tomorrow is thrown into the fire, will he not much more clothe you—you of little faith? So do not worry, saying, 'What shall we eat?' or 'What shall we drink?' or 'What shall we wear?' For the pagans run after all these things, and your heavenly Father knows that you need them. But seek first his kingdom and his righteousness, and all these things will be given to you as well." (Matthew 6:25–33)

"Trust in the LORD with all your heart and lean not on your own understanding; in all your ways submit to him, and he will make your paths straight." (Proverbs 3:5–6)

A Grandmother's Prayer

Lord, as parents and grandparents we want our children and grandchildren to always be healthy and happy, but we live in a world where that is impossible. They will face problems and temptations, just like we do. We pray that you will give them the strength to endure hard times and the humility for when they are blessed with good fortune. Most of all, we pray they will remain faithful to you and look to your word to guide them all the days of their lives. Amen.

Advice from Grandmothers

"If I'm feeling anxious, I always read Philippians 4:6–7. I dissect it and try to apply each part of that verse, because the peace that comes is conditional upon the beginning of the verse. I believe we cannot ask God for anything if we haven't been thankful *before* we make our requests known. Also, the peace that God promises is like a sentinel keeping watch over our mind. That's why it says it will *guard* our hearts and minds. When I think about God's peace guarding my thoughts, it brings me much comfort." —Carol

"Most of the time, I reach for Psalms. They calm me and remind me that God is in control." —Deanna

"I used to be a worrier, but when my son went to Greece with his college class, I felt like God spoke to my heart and said, 'Well, you can't

(continued)

do anything now but trust me.' From that time on, I haven't had a problem with worry. Learning to trust God and give up control is hard. When worry rears its ugly head, I just say a brief prayer: 'Lord, help me to trust you.'" —**Pamela**

"To worry in the Greek language literally means 'to strangle' the life out of you. I still get anxious sometimes, but I literally can't tell you how much my trust has grown in God since I've learned what worry can do to a person." —**Zandra**

"My mother was a worrier. If she didn't have something to worry about, that worried her! I saw her waste a lot of her life in worry, and I made a conscious resolve that I would not live my life that way. Through God's grace and faithfulness, He pulled me up." —**Jimmie**

"Pray, read my Bible or daily devotion, exercise, eat chocolate, go shopping, listen to music, call my best friend. Not necessarily in that order, and often more than once." —**Annette**

"I go hug and hold my precious disabled daughter who has Rett syndrome. She is nonverbal and totally dependent on me. Her eyes speak volumes. I talk to her about everything." —Cindy

"I go to the word and read all the scriptures (again) about worry, trust, and fear. Then I remind myself of a quote I once heard, 'Fear knocked at my door, but Faith refused to open it.'" —Tina

"Spend quiet time in nature. Doesn't take a long time to remember the magnitude of God's power and his faithfulness in promises when you consider that all things work together for those who love him." —Carla

CHAPTER 6

Grandmothers Who Raise Their Grandchildren

No grandparent ever expects to be raising their grandchild, but it happens more frequently than you might think. In the United States alone, 2.7 million grandparents are raising their grandchildren according to PBS,[1] and the numbers continue to rise. Why is this number so high? The main reasons are the opioid epidemic, military deployment, and a rise in the female prison population, according to the Conversation.[2] At a time when

---

1 https://www.pbs.org/newshour/nation/more-grandparents
-raising-their-grandchildren

2 https://theconversation.com/why-more-grandparents-are
-raising-their-grandchildren-83543

most grandparents expect that they will have fewer financial worries and will be able to enjoy retirement, they are finding they can't afford to stay home in order to support themselves and their grandchildren. About one-fifth of these grandparents have incomes that fall below the poverty line. It's no wonder that many of them list worry over their financial situation as one of their top concerns.

And this is only in the United States. In Canada, over 30,000 children ages fourteen and younger live exclusively with their grandparents. This number continues to rise yearly as well. Imagine what the number of grandparents raising grandchildren would be like if we factored in other countries!

Because this phenomenon is so widespread, there is even a term for this situation: *grandfamilies*. Grandfamilies are not new. Maya Angelou, Carol Burnett, and two former presidents, Bill Clinton and Barack Obama, were all raised by a grandmother for at least part of their childhood.

Raising grandchildren is a tough job and often takes a toll on grandparents. Grandparents report depression, sleeplessness, and emotional problems. They give up their privacy and worry about having enough money. Plus, many of them are struggling with their thoughts and feelings toward their adult children who either died or, in most cases, simply deserted their children. Coming to terms with what they expected their retirement to be and how it actually turned out isn't easy.

The grandmothers I spoke with who are raising their grandchildren said that their two biggest problems by far were money and exhaustion. One such grandmother named Louise remarked about the physical toll of being a grandfamily: "I remember being at Walmart to pick up a few things when my granddaughter was around six months old. I walked past the "back to school" supplies and the tears rolled uncontrollably. How am I to do this again? I'm so tired, I am just so TIRED!"

There are organizations and support groups for grandfamilies, but navigating them isn't easy. Laws vary from state to state, and oftentimes the grandparent is so busy just trying to survive that they don't make time to search out what help is available.

Grandfamilies deserve our prayers and help. If you know of grandparents in your church, community, or neighborhood who are raising their grandchildren, why not offer to give them a break occasionally? I'm sure they would love a few hours to go to a movie or maybe just to sleep! If your church family is large, there's a good chance you may not even know who in your congregation is raising their grandchildren. If so, why not investigate and see if there is a need for a grandfamily support group? We should help these grandparents find the resources they need so they can survive and thrive.

The Faith-Filled Grandparent Makes a Difference

Never underestimate the power of a faith-filled grandparent! Remember Timothy? The apostle Paul reminds us that even one parent and/or grandparent can have a major influence on a child.

> "I am reminded of your sincere faith, which first lived in your grandmother Lois and in your mother Eunice and, I am persuaded, now lives in you also." (2 Timothy 1:5)

Grandparents who raise their grandchildren can be like Eunice; they have the chance to influence their grandchildren spiritually every single day.

Each and every grandparent who is raising a grandchild has a story to tell. Their stories will help you better understand what raising grandchildren entails. They are sometimes painful to read, but they help us understand why we need to do a better job of praying for these grandparents and helping them personally through support groups and in any other way we can.

Stories of How Grandmothers Came to Raise Their Grandchildren

Women are by nature "fixers." If someone is upset, we want to make them happy. If someone is ill, we want to help them feel better. If someone is in need of food or clothing, we want to make sure they have enough for their family. But what happens when we run up against something we can't fix?

Many of the women who share their stories below were unable to change the behavior of their adult children, and that brought them sorrow. In almost every example, these grandmothers had to put their heartache aside in order to take control of the situation and meet the needs of their grandchildren. In other words, they couldn't fix their children's problems, but they could rescue their grandchildren from horrible situations.

Here is Jody's story:

So many grandparents share the same story. Our journey started with a phone call where we learned that our granddaughter had been born, and she had been exposed to heroin and cocaine. Her mother had not had any prenatal care, and her father was also an addict. I traveled over a thousand miles to get her fourteen years ago. Our little girl went through multiple seizures. It was gut-wrenching to see such a tiny baby struggle. There are no words to describe the feeling of helplessness and rage at the parents. The hardest thing about being a parent of our grandchild is the isolation and having to navigate schools, doctors, and family court. We refinanced our home twice and we would do it all over again for her. She is now fourteen and an honor student. She is kind and caring and has no behavior problems.

Maureen's story starts in a similar manner:

My son has been the single dad of June, eighteen, and Jason, fourteen, for fourteen years. My daughter-in-law was carjacked and sexually assaulted fifteen years ago, and she has never been the same. She became addicted to pain meds and then heroin.

Jason never had the opportunity to bond with his mom, and the effect of that really started to show the last few years. His sister, June, and my son did their best with him. My poor granddaughter was close to her own nervous breakdown when trying to apply to colleges while keeping her troubled brother on the right path. He is small for his age and was being bullied terribly. The school was not addressing it at all. His mother, who comes and goes, spent one night with them and smoked crack in Jason's room (he has severe asthma). That was it for me. I took custody that morning. He's been with us since January 3, 2018. My son and granddaughter are extremely grateful. My granddaughter is headed to veterinarian school with a full scholarship.

Are you surprised by these two stories? I was, until I kept hearing from more and more grandmothers who shared similar problems, both on NanaHood's Facebook page as well as another Facebook support group for grandmothers raising grandchildren. I quickly learned that this is a much bigger and more serious problem than I had thought.

Barbara helped her daughter raise her grandson from birth. Then, when he was eleven years old, they moved out on their own. Unfortunately, Barbara's daughter started severely abusing him.

Child Protective Services called me and notified me that my grandson was in foster care. For me, there was no alternative. No matter what difficulties I faced, I had to help my grandson. I was granted custody, but it's been hard to get him the help he needs mentally and emotionally and to work through what happened to him. I'm a retired, disabled veteran on a fixed income, but I would do it again. He is finally starting to smile and laugh again.

There is nothing sweeter than the sound of a child's laughter. Can you imagine the pain these children have endured? Very young children especially are not emotionally equipped to deal with such difficult situations. Jesus loves little children, and those who abuse their trust and innocence need our prayers as much as, or even more than, the grandparents who have taken these children into their homes.

Amanda adopted her granddaughter in July of 2018.

She was abused and neglected, and the greatest challenge has been juggling all of her required therapies and doctor appointments with specialists while holding down a full-time job and caring for two step-children who are still living at home. Raising grandchildren is a very long and challenging road, but these children depend on us to take the wheel and redirect their life! I always stay positive and look for the good in everything because children feed off what they see and learn from us. We almost lost this little girl to abuse. Never throw in the towel or give up. I have wondered many times in the last two years if I was going to survive this emotionally, physically, or financially. Then I look at her and realize that I have to survive, not for me but for her.

Have there ever been times in your life when you wondered if you would be able to get through a traumatic event? Where do you turn for comfort and strength?

"Have I not commanded you? Be strong and courageous. Do not be afraid; do not be discouraged, for the Lord your God will be with you wherever you go." (Joshua 1:9)

God won't leave us or forsake us, ever. That's a comforting promise in times of trouble.

Beth tells her story:

Shane's parents voluntarily placed him in our custody before he turned two because of addiction on my son's part, and Shane's mother just didn't want to be a mom. Shane has been in counseling since 2013. It helps him deal with issues of abandonment by his Mom and Dad. The greatest reward is watching him grow into a young man who has such a kind, loving nature. His counselor says he has integrity, which makes me very proud. He makes good grades and is well-adjusted. Most important, he is growing into a good, young, Christian man.

How does it make us feel as grandparents when someone gives our grandchild a compliment? How do we respond? When my children were very young my pediatrician told me to try to remember to "catch them being good." Reinforcing good behavior is so important. Now when I see my grandchildren doing a good deed or exhibiting exceptionally thoughtful behavior I think of her advice and give them praise for what they did. I try to make it specific to the deed and then remind them that they are behaving like Jesus when they help others. When I read them Bible stories I try to point out how many times Jesus reached out to the less fortunate and those in need.

Virginia explains how she came to raise her grandchildren:

> We came to be raising my three grands because my daughter is an addict. She was shooting meth and was homeless—and still is along with the kids' biological father. They both went to rehab last year with the agreement that she could bring the kids and stay with us until she got back on her feet. There were also some arrests and probation issues. The dad showed up a couple weeks after she arrived; they had no car and no jobs. By July we were forced to legally evict them. They finally left with the agreement that they would find a place (at this point, both had jobs and we helped my daughter get her license reinstated and a car). They were doing drugs the entire time they were being supported by us. I still had hope that she would straighten up, but she didn't. In March of this year, we filed for full custody and they did not contest it. We were granted custody in June.

We don't ever want to give up hope when it comes to our adult children, but they have to want to help themselves. We can suggest treatment and programs for their addictions, but we cannot force them to do anything they don't want to do. It's heartbreaking to watch them destroy their lives, but the least we can do is to give our grandchildren a chance for a life of their own. If these grandmothers (and grandfathers) hadn't been willing to take action, their grandchildren would not have that chance.

Here is Louise's story:

I was a stay-at-home mom who'd raised four children. Just a few years into experiencing "life after children," my youngest son (twenty-three years old) told me his fiancé was pregnant. My first grandchild was born in January 2015, four weeks early. At three days old, she was transported from the "birth hospital" to Akron Children's Hospital. Her parents fabricated a reason as to why she was there and couldn't be visited by other family members including myself. Finally, I forced my way with the parents into allowing me to see my grandbaby, who was still in NICU (neonatal intensive care unit) at two weeks old.

The situation was becoming suspicious. In that same week, I received a call from CPS (child protection services) asking if I was willing and able to take emergency shelter care of her. In my own heart and mind, there was nothing to consider. She was my grandbaby. I couldn't even entertain the thought of allowing her to go into foster care. At this point, I knew some sort of drugs had been involved.

I soon learned my granddaughter was born drug dependent (heroin). I was sickened and devastated to say the least; I just couldn't wrap my head around this news. We had a court hearing to place her with me under emergency shelter care with temporary custody to follow. Later, a reunification program was put in place.

I was working a full-time job and had one week to prepare for this new little life that I had just met, not knowing what, if any, damage had been done by the drug exposure. We decided it would be best that I quit my job to be home with the baby. By June 2015, the parents were still not able to stay clean. I felt it best for my granddaughter that I file for custody. I was granted sole custody in July, 2015.

Some of the difficulties of raising a grandchild are the changing of gears. You have your own thoughts and dreams of what you want to do with your life once your children become adults. My most exciting plan was to buy a motorcycle. That was actually to happen the spring following the birth of my granddaughter. Now, I jokingly say I'd planned on getting a motorcycle but got a stroller instead!

Have you ever heard the quote, "Man plans, God laughs"? Life has a way of handing us surprises.

How do we react when we expect one thing but are given another? Many of us have dreams of a peaceful, problem-free retirement; but that's not always the case.

Remember the parable of the rich fool? He decided he would tear down his barns and build bigger ones to store his grain in. There was nothing wrong with that, but his attitude was not right. Instead of being grateful for what he had been given, he said, "'And I'll say to myself, "You have plenty of grain laid up for many years. Take life easy; eat, drink and be merry."' But God said to him, 'You fool! This very night your life will be demanded from you. Then who will get what you have prepared for yourself?' This is how it will be with whoever stores up things for themselves but is not rich toward God" (Luke 12:19-21).

We have to expect the unexpected. Nothing in this earthly life is guaranteed. God doesn't promise us that this life will be easy, but he promises us the reward of Heaven if we have a grateful heart and trust in Him.

Sheila shares her story and the challenges she faced:

I don't know that others even consider the full picture of raising a grandchild. They think of it as if it were simply the act of raising a child, but I doubt they consider the stress, fear, and heartbreak of the circumstances, as many of us are raising these babies due to the addiction epidemic. Not only do you have all the difficulties of dealing with your adult child's addiction—the disbelief that *your* child had turned to drugs, all the lies, and the fear of that one dose that would potentially take their life as you helplessly watch your child fade away— BUT you also now have a new baby to care for, and to raise to adulthood in many cases.

This brings on a whole slew of concerns. Many babies who are born drug dependent are adversely affected with poor sleep patterns, ADHD, anger issues, separation anxiety, sensory issues—some of which are not seen until school age—and the list goes on. Not to mention that this child is going to be emotionally affected by the knowledge of why they are being raised by their grandparents rather than their parents.

On the lighter side, but still something I struggle with sometimes, is the fact that I don't really get to be the grandparent. I don't get to spoil her and send her home. She doesn't get to pack up and spend the night with us as grandparents. It's kind of reversed—her parents get to come over, visit her, bring her treats or whatever else, and then they go about their lives. They get to go to concerts, hang out with friends . . . they even get to shower whenever they want!

Now, the upside of raising a grandchild . . . this is where I am at a loss for words. With great sacrifice comes greater rewards. She is the very beat of my heart and my every breath. She's my little sidekick, my precious angel. What I have given up to raise her pales in comparison to what I have gained. When she wraps those little arms around me and says, "Gwamie, I love you," I know without a doubt that my life has purpose. My goal is to raise her in a way that her life story will give her strength rather than be a weakness. I hope to teach her for-giveness, compassion, and the ability to love without measure. I hope to instill in her the notion that we get to choose to take seem-ingly negative circumstances or life events and use them to grow, to be strengthened, and to become a better person.

Have you noticed that every story so far features moments of pain as well as joy?

One of my favorite singers and performers was Jim Croce. Sadly, he was killed at a very young age in a plane crash, but what a gift he left behind with his music! One of my favorite Jim Croce songs says, "Nobody ever had a rainbow baby until they had the rain." These grandmothers have certainly had rain in their lives, but their grandchildren bring them rainbows.

Kim is another grandmother who raises her grandkids.

We are raising our grandson, eleven, and our granddaughter, nine. They have been with us on and off since birth, whenever our daugh-ter wasn't withholding them and playing emotional blackmail with us. Her life was, and is, very dysfunctional. She is addicted to opiates. She would land wherever she could with her kids, couch surfing or sleeping on floors, or she would leave them with strangers for days or weeks. She lived two states away and would never give us an address. The final straw was when the kids, then ages three and four, were found alone in a park at 11 p.m. while she was passed out at home. Long story short, that is when the children came to live with us "temporarily" until she took steps to straighten out her life. After three years of almost zero contact, we adopted the kids.

It has now been over six years and nothing has changed. Our daughter has become so abusive to us that we have had to block all contact or communication. When the kids first came to live with us, they were basically like feral cats. They weren't potty trained, were barely verbal, and were both diagnosed with RAD (reactive attachment disorder) and ODD (oppositional defiant disorder). Our grandson was also diagnosed with ADHD and is on the autism spectrum. We found an amazing therapist and she worked wonders. They are still afraid of open closets, open curtains in their bedrooms, strangers, crowds, and a fear that she or one of her friends will take them. They remember things that no child should ever have had to live through, and that breaks my heart.

Janet shares:

We were forced into doing an intervention with our daughter when our granddaughter was just four years old. Our daughter was out of control. She left my granddaughter on a street corner when she was seven years old and told her I was coming to get her. Eventually we adopted our granddaughter and moved to a different state for her protection in 2015. Three years later, our daughter overdosed on meth.

Finally, Melinda says:

I have had my granddaughter since she was three months old. She is now in pre-K and is almost five. Both birth parents are in prison. The birth father has only seen her once. My granddaughter will be almost eighteen by the time her birth mother (my only child) is released from prison.

The greatest challenge is not being able to spoil her and be a grandmother. I have to discipline her and not let her have that cookie at bedtime; I have to make her brush her teeth and clean her room.

The most rewarding thing is that little dimply-faced girl who hugs me so tight and tells me she loves me out of the blue at least twenty times a day.

No matter what their personal circumstances, these grandmothers have risen to the challenges presented to them. They have chosen to put their grandchildren's wants and needs ahead of their own. Isn't that what Jesus did so many times? There were moments when he was weary and moments when he was treated unfairly. There were times when he was disappointed in his friends and times when he just had to get away from it all and pray to God. Yet, he didn't give up. He pressed on and did the will of his Father.

One of my dad's favorite church hymns was "One Day at a Time." When life becomes wearisome, remember to take things one day at a time. Press on, like Jesus did. He will carry you through.

God's Promises

No matter what challenges you face, you can be certain of God's promise:

> "Be strong and courageous. Do not be afraid or terrified because of them, for the Lord your God goes with you; he will never leave you nor forsake you."
> (Deuteronomy 31:6)

Grandparents who raise their grandchildren are leaving an amazing inheritance of time, effort, and love.

> "A good man leaves an inheritance to his children's children."
> (Proverbs 13:22, NASB)

A Grandmother's Prayer

Lord God, we love and praise you for the blessings our grandchildren bring to our lives. There are so many problems in our society today, and we want to train and bring up our children and grandchildren in the right way— but we need your help. Give us strength and patience to deal with the problems that arise. Comfort our aching hearts when our children make mistakes that keep them from being the parents their children need them to be. Show us the way to live so that we might influence our children and grandchildren to develop spiritually and avoid the evil temptations of the world. Amen.

Advice from Grandmothers

"Hold on and enjoy the ride. You will not remember it ever being this hard when you were younger and raising your first family; the money goes quick and grandkids *always* need something. But oh, the rewards will always outweigh the struggles. I would do it all over again a thousand times. My granddaughter is my life, my only reason to be able to go on when my daughter turned to drugs and then received a twenty-year prison sentence. It was no accident that she was given to me at the right time in life. She is a blessing." —**Melinda**

"My advice (in such situations) is to step in. Don't wait—it won't get better. My guilt weighs heavily on me for allowing my daughter to use my grandchildren as pawns. You live and learn. This has been extremely hard on my marriage as well." —**Virginia**

(continued)

"My advice for anyone going through something similar would be to document everything in case you try to gain custody. To this day, there is no parental involvement in my grandchildren. The anger and rage I had are gone. Now I am only sad for her parents. They missed a lot of wonderful memories." —Jody

"One of the hardest things is to step out of the spoiling and fun grandparent role and step into the responsible parenting role. It's tough, especially because we have twelve other grandkids. Jimmy, the grandson we are raising, is fourteen years old. My husband and I talked about it, and we decided that when we are on adventures with the other grandkids, we will be our regular grandparent selves, but at home we are in charge of helping him grow into the best man possible. I would also advise having the best support system you can put together. Our other kids have really stepped up as aunts and uncles, and they've included Justin in their vacations, which gives us a few nice breaks over the summer." —Doris

"Document everything, every message between you and the parents, and then print it out. Do a memo and record every conversation. Don't assume that people are on your side. You will be surprised. You may find out you don't really know your grandchild's parents, even if they are your own kids. I found out so much about my daughter that I found hard to believe until they showed me the evidence. I had to begin counseling and had to realize the daughter I knew no longer existed; it was as if she had died. She will never be who she was again. Be prepared for anything and be ready to go to war, to fight the battle of a lifetime. Your mission is to save your grandchild!" —**Barbara**

"Seek out every service you can. Try to find parents your age. Join a group and be active with your grandchildren. They are tons of fun!" —**Nancy**

"My advice is patience. These children come with hurts and issues. You have to be a parent. You have to listen to them as they learn how to voice their hurts. Be ready for the question, 'Why would God give me to parents like mine?' Also, their classmates may ask, 'What did you do to make your mom leave?' Raising

(continued)

a grandchild is harder than raising a child. There is a lot of heartache, but the joy that follows outweighs the bad!" —Beth

"Hang on! You will shed a lot of tears and feel a lot of guilt about your adult child. Stay focused on what is best for everyone, especially the children. Just when you think you cannot take one more second of all the craziness, fall to your knees and ask God for help and guidance." —Kim

"I'm not sure what advice I could give to someone just beginning their journey in raising grandchildren other than to take it one day at a time. Don't get too caught up in deep thought of a year from now, five years from now, or heaven forbid you think of the teen years! Sadly, we are not the minority anymore; you are certainly not alone. Something I like to keep in mind is that I have the most important, special job in the whole world, and I am determined that I can and will make a positive difference in this child's life! As to the question of "Would I do it again?" YES! A million times over, and I pray each and every time that I do it well." —Patty

"My advice would be to put your grandchildren first no matter what. Your children are adults and can make their own decisions; your grandchildren can't. Don't hesitate to do everything in your power to protect them." —Diane

CHAPTER 7

Grandparents Who Aren't Allowed to See Their Grandchildren

*I*n an ideal world, a baby would be welcomed into a loving two-parent home, with two sets of adoring grandparents. In this utopia, the child would grow up surrounded by parents, grandparents, and cousins. Everyone would get along, and there would be no dissension or divisions between family members. Too often, that's not the way things work.

These grandmothers know firsthand what it feels like to be kept from their grandchildren, and their stories are heartbreaking.

Glenna tells her story:

My son moved in with his girlfriend, Mavis, immediately after his release from prison for drug trafficking. Mavis already had two children and quickly became pregnant with my grandchild. Eventually they had two children together. My son gets busted for drugs again and goes back to prison. I am an LPN (licensed practical nurse), and I'm raising another granddaughter from my other son. I've had her since she was fifteen months old.

At this point Mavis starts asking me for money while my son is still in prison. When I couldn't meet all her demands, she stopped letting me see the children. She moves from city to city and works as a dancer. I have no idea who watches the kids, and it's been two years since I've seen them. It eats at me every day. I am strong in my faith, active in church, and my oldest grandchild keeps me busy with school, sports, and piano; but the void is still there. I miss my grandchildren every day and I'm scared for their safety. I have two wonderful friends at work who are in similar situations.

Becky adds her experience into the mix.

> My daughter doesn't allow me to see my grandson. She says it's because they only want him bonding with them (the parents). I want to support them, but everything feels extreme and I am beyond sad. My husband and I have asked how sharing love with the baby could be a bad thing. We have no control. I don't know if other grandparents have dealt with this, but I'm hurting.

Rachel says:

> My daughter and I are estranged because of my daughter's substance abuse. I have not seen my grandchildren since early December of last year. I pray and talk to friends and try not to think about it, but that doesn't work. I feel ashamed because I feel like I am less than a good mother and nana. To have them gone from my life has created such a void that will never be filled unless their mother has a change of heart. I would say that this type of estrangement is as deep as mourning a death.

Shana shares:

> I call myself an "erased" grandmother. My two oldest grandchildren have been brainwashed by their custodial parent. They live with their father, and he remains on a revenge-driven path to hurt my daughter by using the kids to hate her. I could go on and on about this heartbreaking situation, but at the end of the day I miss them very much.

These grandmothers are not alone. In fact, there are thousands of them around, though no one knows exactly how many because they are often ashamed and prefer to keep their relationship problems with their adult children to themselves.

Kim, another grandmother who is not allowed to see her grandchildren, adds, "Being reluctant to talk about the estrangement only isolates grandparents more. In opening up to a couple of people, I found out they were going through the exact same thing."

Remember the story of the prodigal son in the Bible? I knew the story well, or so I thought. Luke 15:11–32 tells the parable of an ungrateful son who demands his inheritance from his father. His father gives it to him and the son leaves home, spending all the money on foolish things. Finally, he exhausts it all to the point that he finds himself feeding pigs for a living, wishing he could eat the pig food. Recently, when I read verse 17, I realized I'd never noticed the words used in the first part of the verse: *"When he came to his senses,* he said, 'How many of my father's hired servants have food to spare, and here I am starving to death!'" The young man went back to his father who welcomed him home with open arms.

But he didn't go home until *"he came to his senses"* (emphasis mine).

The Financial and Emotional Costs of a Legal Battle

When something goes wrong between adult children and their parents, there are only a few options available to repair the relationship. If one or the other party isn't willing to compromise (or come to their senses), then the situation isn't going to change.

There are legal options available and grandparents do have some rights in most states. But two things to consider if you choose to engage in a long and drawn-out court battle are its financial costs and emotional impact.

Unfortunately, there is no way to know for sure how much legal fees are going to cost. Every lawyer has different rates and there's no way to know how many hours you will be billed for. The cost of a legal battle can add up to thousands of dollars in a very short time.

As for the emotional impact, Marianne is a grandmother who knows all too well the cost of fighting for her grandchild. She and her husband, Jeff, have been in and out of the court system for years trying to keep their grandson, Alex, in their home.

Sadly, their son, Alex's father, had died, and Alex's mother had a drug problem. She gave Alex to his grandparents. However, without legal documentation, she simply showed up from time to time to take him with her. Invariably, he'd usually end up back at Marianne and Jeff's house, confused, exhausted, and usually hungry and dirty. Just when Marianne thought they'd be able to convince the courts that Alex's mom is an unfit parent, she refiled in another court.

"It has cost us a fortune and been the hardest fight of my life but I'm not giving up," Marianne says. "I just can't give up because of what it would do to Alex. This has been so hard on all of us. The things Alex's mother accused us of in court were out-and-out lies, but they were so painful to listen to that I had to start taking medication. My nerves are a wreck and Jeff's aren't much better.

We live in a small community and everyone knows us. Being accused of unspeakable crimes doesn't make us guilty, but it's embarrassing and some people we thought were friends look at us differently now."

Grandmothers Who Are Alienated

When you aren't allowed to see your grandchildren, you're sure to experience a profound sense of loss. Often, it triggers a grieving process very similar to what happens when a loved one dies (see Chapter 9, "Grandmothers Who Grieve").

While you may not experience all the five stages of grief, there is a good chance you will go through most of them if the separation from your grandchild continues for a prolonged period. These stages vary in length and order with each individual. Some of us may experience more of one stage than another, and we may go back and forth from one stage to another. We will discuss each one of the stages in between the grandmothers' accounts of their alienation from their grandchildren.

Below, story after story is shared by grandmothers with broken hearts. If this is happening to you, you are definitely not alone! Seek out support groups at your place of worship, in your community, and online. There is always hope.

1. Denial and Isolation

When someone who has been in our lives is no longer there, we may experience an unwillingness to believe that this is really happening. It seems impossible to think that someone we love so much (our child) would intentionally cause us pain. There is a surreal feeling that isolates us as we try to deal with the loss of contact with our grandchild. This is a coping mechanism that gets us through the first stage of grief.

Here is Sylvia's story:

My oldest daughter was diagnosed with alopecia areata that attacked her ovaries so she could not have children the conventional way. She looked into invitro fertilization and asked her younger sister if she would be willing to donate eggs. She agreed. The results were a baby boy, who is seven, and a baby girl, who is five. I truly believe this has played a huge part in the estrangement because if anything ever didn't go my oldest daughter's way, her first reaction was to keep the children from their aunt. I believe my oldest daughter is jealous of her younger sister's ability to produce and donate eggs, which was a selfless thing she'd done.

Now, my oldest daughter has completely removed them from my husband's and my life. She has welcomed everyone back but myself and my husband. We aren't invited to birthdays or holidays anymore. The last time we were all together was Easter 2016. That day, my husband and our youngest granddaughter were playing their usual game—she would run away every time Grandpa asked for a hug. She would hide and peek around corners, laughing, and waiting for Grandpa to ask her when she was going to give him a hug. Our granddaughter's father decided this was improper. He stated that it's her body and that she doesn't have to do anything she doesn't want to. Something so sweet between a Grandpa and his granddaughter, a playtime ritual, was made out to be something so ugly. Our son-in-law went on social media to say that my husband was forcing himself on his little girl. I've never in my life thought anyone could be so completely wrong and hateful about something so innocent. They left and we were told we could not see the grandkids anymore. This was the third time they had removed them from our lives.

How do I cope? It has been excruciating. I've had to take down all the pictures I have of them. I pray every day and every night that our grandkids will not think we hate them. I stay busy.

Grandma L shares:

I haven't been able to see my youngest son's two children for almost two years.

My son has blocked his immediate family from all social media, emails, texts, or phone calls. He told me that the reason he doesn't want to talk to me is because he says I lied to him about some money I gave to my oldest son. The money was from my father who was dying at the time, and it was his (my father's) wish that I give the money to my oldest son, who was the apple of my dad's eye.

Now I'm just lost. I live in Ohio where we have no grandparent rights. My estranged son is a Marine and currently stationed in another state. I cry a lot and write letters to the two grandchildren every week. One day I hope I will be able to give them the letters and cards I've written.

In Sylvia's and Grandma L's stories, there is an element of jealousy between two siblings. Jealousy has caused problems in families since the beginning of time. In fact, the first murder reported in the Bible was between two brothers, Cain and Abel. Cain was jealous that God preferred Abel's offering. "Now Cain said to his brother Abel, 'Let's go out to the field.' While they were in the field, Cain attacked his brother Abel and killed him" (Genesis 4:8).

In Sylvia's story, one daughter is jealous of the other due to fertility problems. In Grandma L's case, one brother is jealous of another over a gift. There are many things that are out of our control as parents and grandparents. While we can't prevent jealousies forming between siblings, we can do our best to treat each child and grandchild the same. Even the perception of favoritism can give root to jealousy.

2. Anger

I doubt there is a person alive who hasn't experienced anger at one time or another. But when anger is directed at a family member, it can be exceptionally intense. If we aren't careful, anger can cause us to say or do things that can make a bad situation much worse.

We are warned of the damage anger can do in the book of James. "Wherefore, my beloved brethren, let every man be swift to hear, slow to speak, slow to wrath: For the wrath of man worketh not the righteousness of God" (James 1:19–20, KJV).

When my mother was diagnosed with terminal cancer, I was extremely angry at her doctor for misdiagnosing her stomach problems as depression. Colon cancer is one of the most curable types of cancer if it is caught early. By the time her doctor found what was really wrong with her, it was too late. She was only fifty-one years old when she died. I blamed her doctor for her death and gave serious thought to confronting him and telling him what I thought, but I never did for several reasons. First, it was pointless—it wouldn't have brought my mother back. Second, my mother was a grown woman; she could have gone to any doctor she wanted to, but she chose him. She was his patient by choice, not necessity.

It took me years before I was able to let go of my anger. I finally realized it was a wasted emotion. It wasn't changing anything, and the only person I was hurting was myself.

There are a multitude of Bible verses about anger, but one of the most applicable when it comes to grandparent alienation may be, "A soft answer turneth away wrath: but grievous words stir up anger" (Proverbs 15:1, KJV).

Nana K tells her story:

My firstborn child, my daughter, estranged herself from the family three weeks before my first grandchild, a granddaughter, was born. I thought my daughter and I had a great relationship, so this came out of the blue. She refuses to talk to me or tell me why she's upset. She says things like I was never there for her, that I put my wants before her needs, etc. I learned about the birth of my granddaughter from a group text with twenty other people. I didn't even know my daughter was in labor, and I was banned from the hospital after her birth. My granddaughter was in the NICU for nine days, and my daughter refused to tell me why. She was born in January of 2016, and I still have not met her. My daughter also cut off contact with my husband (her stepfather of twenty-six years), her younger half-brother, and her maternal grandmother.

Because of this sudden estrangement, I suffer from a mixture of complicated grief, ambiguous loss, and emotional trauma. This has led to bouts of anxiety and avoidance of social situations. I did complete eight sessions of therapy earlier this year that helped relieve the anxiety for about three months, but it has recently started to reoccur.

Grandma K explains her situation:

My daughter-in-law filed for divorce from my son in 2017. At first, she just stopped answering phone calls or returning my texts about my four granddaughters. In a normal month, we would see them at least eight or ten times and have sleepovers, too. They live about ten miles from me, and I would pick them up for cheer practice or dance lessons. Visits started getting cut out, and at Christmas last year we were only allowed to visit them at their house for thirty minutes. Then we stopped getting invited to their birthday parties.

This summer, I saw the girls at a soccer game (our grandson from our daughter also plays). When I approached my daughter-in-law to talk to them, she yelled at me to get away. The next week, she made them quit soccer. I had been paying for one of the girls to take dance classes, but on the day of the recital she didn't show up. We have had no contact with them since March of this year.

Additionally, my son will not allow us to see them because he doesn't want his ex-wife to get mad. He is not dealing well with the divorce. I have started therapy and that is helping some.

3. Bargaining or "What If . . . ?"

After my mother died, I experienced horrible guilt. I wondered, "What if I had made her go to a different doctor? What if I had paid more attention to her health problems? What if I had gotten her to a doctor sooner?" I nearly drove myself crazy wondering how I could have prevented her death.

When alienation occurs, we may wonder, "What if I had done this or that differently?" But the truth is we can't change the past. Worrying over something we did or did not do isn't going to make a difference.

We need to recognize that this is a normal reaction caused by grief and that we have little or no control over what others say, do, or think. If your child is denying you time with your grandchild, focus on what you can do instead of what you can't. Suggestions for coping are at the end of this chapter.

Lana's shares her story, and explains how therapy has helped her:

My daughter was married to a narcissistic psychopath for ten years. She changed and became just like him. My husband and I believed that if she ever left him, we would have our daughter back. We were wrong.

During the marriage, my daughter had two children. We babysat them all the time, including the summers when I was off. We took them on vacations. We provided clothing and meals. We took them to school and daycare and picked them up. When my daughter left her husband, we were there for support. We took her into our home and for two years gave them a free place to live, eat, etc. But soon, our daughter began acting very oddly, and things started to escalate. One day, we came home to find that all their belongings were gone. They had moved thousands of miles away. We never got to say goodbye.

That was eight years ago. At first, we were allowed limited contact with our grandchildren. I tried to talk to them on the phone and sent them letters and packages. That lasted for about three months. Then everything I'd sent was mailed back with a "return to sender" mark on them. Our daughter did email her father once, telling him that I was the cause of all this and that she needed to protect her kids from me. She goes to great lengths to make sure we don't know where they are.

At first, I did not cope well at all. I had never felt so much sorrow and pain. I cried all the time. I went to the hospital with issues that they thought were symptomatic of a heart attack. I finally went into therapy, trying to fix what was wrong with me. The therapists I talked to told me I wasn't the problem, but I was sure I must be. Why else would my own daughter do what she had done?

I was very depressed and pulled away from my family and friends. I prayed a lot. I wrote in a journal to my grandchildren, and I put the things they had given me in a box for them to receive when I die. I took all photos down as I could not bear looking at them. Those I could talk to got sick of hearing my problems.

One day I got tired of hiding. I started making an effort to be honest whenever someone asked me about my daughter or grandchildren. I found Dr. Josh Coleman, psychologist and speaker on family estrangements, and his weekly Q and A sessions, which are free online (www.drjoshuacoleman.com).

I learned that I'm not the only one this has happened to. There are thousands like me. I started a Facebook page in case my grandchildren ever want to find me. Each birthday I write something to them. Little by little, I realized that although I am not perfect, this issue is not about me and my problems.

My suggestion to others in this situation is to find as many resources as you can. There are more and more available. Take care of yourself. Find people or a group who will listen and understand. Quit beating yourself up. Parents make mistakes, but most of us do the best we can do. Time will not make things better, but the work you do for yourself will make life tolerable.

4. Depression

Anyone who has ever experienced severe depression will tell you it can be debilitating. Elaine, a close friend of mine, was diagnosed with clinical depression many years ago.

"There are days when I find it hard to get out of bed in the morning. I just want to pull the covers up over my head and sleep forever," she says. "Instead I make myself get up and keep going. I start every day with Bible study, prayer, and lots of coffee!"

Depression can cause sadness, tearfulness, emptiness, or feelings of hopelessness.

I have often joked that I could have been a professional mourner because of my ability to cry. I'm just a softie, and it doesn't take much to bring the tears. I've been known to shed tears over Hallmark commercials! In other countries, it was once common to hire people to wail and cry at funerals. Why anyone would want to do that, I don't know. Crying is exhausting, and so is being depressed.

There is a big difference between feeling sad and experiencing intense depression. According to Mayo Clinic, here are some symptoms of depression:[1]

- If you are overly irritable and angry, especially if you are usually easygoing by nature.
- If all the things you once enjoyed no longer bring you pleasure.
- If you suffer from sleep problems. One of my friends who suffers from depression has trouble sleeping and prowls around her house all hours of the night; another friend can't get out of bed.

---

1   www.mayoclinic.org/diseases-conditions/depression /symptoms-causes/syc-20356007

- If you find yourself feeling sluggish and tired all the time.
- If you have problems with your appetite: some people experience weight gain while others lose weight and find it hard to eat.
- If you are experiencing brain fog: to me, it feels like the wheels and cogs in my brain are barely turning. For example, I had a hard time making decisions because my thought process felt like it was moving in slow motion.

Of all the stages of grief, depression can be the most serious and the hardest to deal with. If you experience several of the symptoms above, don't be afraid to seek help. Your doctor or therapist can help you work through your problems.

And don't forget who is considered to be "The Great Physician." Jesus Christ intercedes for us. He hears you and makes your needs known to the Father.

"Consequently, he is able to save to the uttermost those who draw near to God through him, since he always lives to make intercession for them." (Hebrews 7:25, ESV)

Despite Etrecia's struggles, she vows to give it up to God.

> I saw my grandson last in 2013 when my son and his ex-partner broke up. Then, he left her and his son for Cape Town, South Africa. Every attempt to get in contact with my grandson has been refused by his mother with aggressiveness, bitterness, and silence. I still cannot cope with this situation. The court refused to hear my case and chased me out of the court room. The school my grandson is attending is treating me like a criminal, and his mother refuses to let me give him even a birthday present.
>
> Some days I just want to let go, but life is never fair. Sometimes it is difficult to pray for my grandson's mother. All we can do is to leave it in our Almighty Lord God's hands. Grandchildren grow up and eventually start asking questions.

If you are a grandparent who is not allowed to see your grandchildren, remember that Jesus can and will help you through each and every crisis in your life.

God's Promises

"Blessed are those who mourn, for they will be comforted." (Matthew 5:4)

"So do not fear, for I am with you; do not be dismayed, for I am your God. I will strengthen you and help you; I will uphold you with my righteous right hand." (Isaiah 41:10)

Knowing Jesus doesn't stop us from hurting, but trusting in him brings peace that surpasses all understanding. When we have problems we may not feel like we are blessed at that time, but we can trust in his promise that we can find comfort in him.

A Grandmother's Prayer

God, help us to trust in your word, especially when our hearts are breaking. We know you understand and we know you love us. You gave your only son for our sins, and that was the ultimate sacrifice. Hear our prayer, oh Lord, and if it be your will please guide our path and that of our adult children so that we can once again have peace in our family and have our grandchildren back in our lives. Your will be done in all things, Lord, and give us strength to endure whatever your will may be. Amen.

Advice from Grandmothers

"My advice for other alienated grandparents: write to your grandchildren in a journal. Attach photos. Get them cards for every birthday and holiday. Tell them you never stopped loving them. Talk to someone. It helps a lot."
—Sylvia

"Don't allow yourself to give into anger or say something that could make matters worse."
—Cheryl

"Realize the situation is out of your control. You cannot force a change in the behavior of others. I have trouble with this one. I think if I keep talking I can convince them . . . anyone else think that?" —Beth

"Channel your energies into positive activities that will make a difference in someone's life, even if they will not solve your problems."
—Susan

"Don't give up hope. Keep trying to mend the broken relationship." —Sara

"Create a 'Someday Box.' Put letters and gifts and notes in it to give to your grandchild someday." —Lara

"Find someone you can talk to and grieve with. Friend. Therapist. Minister. You are NOT alone." —Ana

"My advice is never give up. I pray every day for Mavis (my son's girlfriend) and her salvation and a softening of her heart. I have contacted multiple attorneys with no luck because I have no money. I have reached out to my state representatives and I have emailed, messaged, and written to Mavis and her mom. I keep every response. I also take pictures of every card I have ever sent them, along with the UPS postage receipt. I will continue to do this. When I die, my will states that my grandchildren will get this information so they will know the truth about how their mother treated me, their cousin, and their family. I want them to know I never turned my back on them and that I will not give up until I take my last breath!" —Glenna

CHAPTER 8

Grandmothers Who Grieve

Children and grandchildren bring us so much joy, but the same source of that happiness also has the potential to crush us with sorrow. There is a quote in A. A. Milne's *Winnie the Pooh* that says, "If you live to be a hundred, I want to live to be a hundred minus one day so I never have to live without you." That pretty much sums up how parents and grandparents feel about their children and grandchildren.

Nothing is sadder than the death of a grandchild. This traumatic event doesn't just mean losing a precious grandchild; it also means grandparents have to see their own son or daughter experience unfathomable sorrow. Grandparents often try to be strong for their children, even when their own heart is breaking. They worry: will their child ever recover from such a loss? How will a death affect their child's marriage or the siblings of the grandchild? How will their family ever get through the holidays and birthdays with a grandchild missing?

There are no easy answers to questions like these. We all handle grief differently. Most important, when we have friends and family who experience unspeakable tragedies, we need to be there for them in whatever form or fashion they need us to be.

If there is one thing I learned while working on this book, it is that many grandmothers have an ache in their hearts. Those who are not allowed to see their grandchildren, those whose children who are drug dependent, those who are dealing with a child's infertility, those whose children have moved away . . . we are all dealing with some sort of loss.

Remember Job from the Bible? Probably no one experienced more catastrophes in such a short time as he did. He lost all his belongings and his children—all of them. His grief must have been unbearable, but one of the things about his story that has always amazed me is that when Job's friends heard what happened, they traveled to be with him. They could barely recognize him, and they were so upset at his appearance and his deep, deep sadness that they "sat on the ground with him for seven days and seven nights. No one said a word to him, because they saw how great his suffering was" (Job 2:13).

Can you imagine sitting with someone for a week and not saying a word? I think most of us would find it impossible. Yet that's what Job needed. We also forget in our rush to comfort someone that sometimes silence is better. There simply are no words of comfort at certain times. Just holding a hand or being the shoulder they can lean on may be way more important than trying to figure out what to say.

Often, it's not what we say that will bring the most comfort anyway; it's what we do.

Years ago, I read a story in a magazine that I've never forgotten:

A woman received a phone call from her mother, telling her that her brother, his wife, and their two children had been killed in a car accident. The mother asked her daughter to come as soon as she could. As the woman hung up the phone, she described the feeling of being frozen. She couldn't think. She couldn't move. She just sat and tried to comprehend what her mother had just said. The woman was married and had two children herself, and there was much to be done to prepare for the trip back to her home state. Her husband made the plane reservations as she stumbled through the rooms of her house trying to think but feeling like she was in a fog. Hours later, someone knocked on their door. It was a friend from her church, not someone they knew particularly well, but well enough that they recognized him as a quiet, unassuming man who had a wife and a passel of loud children. "I've come to clean your shoes," he announced.

The woman shook her head, not understanding. He repeated his mission. His wife was home with the children and he said they wanted to help. When his father had died, someone had come to his house and cleaned his shoes.

The woman hadn't even thought about shoes. She could barely remember what items of clothing they would need for the trip. She went and got her children's good shoes (which were dirty from playing in a muddy field), her heels, and her husband's dress shoes.

The man took them and asked for a pan of water, soap, something to scrub with, and shoe polish. Then he told her to get the rest of their shoes. He wanted to do them all—and he did.

The lesson the woman learned from the man who washed their shoes was one that we all need to remember. Whenever someone loses a loved one, don't call with a vague offer of "if there's anything

I can do." Instead, go wash their car, take their dog to the boarding kennel, or house sit during the funeral. Be the man who cleans the shoes—because he was following the man who washed his disciples' feet.

Stories from Grieving Grandmothers

Susan shares the story of her daughter's miscarriage:

My concern for my daughter outweighed the grief that I felt at losing my precious grandchild. In a state of deep grief, she rarely left the couch for days on end as the miscarriage was allowed to run its course naturally, in God's timing. It was a long and heart-wrenching process. I held her hand, listened to her when she felt like talking, reassured her that we would get through this together. I prayed that God would watch over her, help her, and heal her. I took care of practical matters like grocery shopping, cooking, cleaning, and laundry so that she and her husband could focus on grieving, recovering, and finding the strength to move forward. Because they had faced years of infertility before this pregnancy, this was an especially bitter pill for them to swallow. My advice to other grandmothers is to remember that every miscarriage is different and each brings with it unique needs.

Ellie speaks about the death of her granddaughter:

My sixth grandchild was stillborn, past full-term. Her mom, my daughter-in-law, had had no problems during the entire pregnancy and had a perfect checkup the day before. But one evening she was worried because she wasn't feeling the baby moving. They went to the hospital in the middle of the night. Their firstborn baby, Elliot Kathryn Davis, had no heartbeat. The next morning was a nightmare. My poor son had to call and give us the news. At the time he called we happened to be at our other daughter's (his sister's) house, taking care of their two older girls while she, coincidentally, was also in the hospital delivering her third child. On her first morning home, when she expected to find out she had a new niece, we had to tell her and my son-in-law that the baby had died. Then we threw some clothes on and raced to be with my son and wife. We stayed with them in the hospital for the three days it took for her to have the baby. Heartbreaking is not a sufficient word. This event changed us forever. It was extremely sad, but it was also a moment that showed us we were in God's hands.

Our family has done an exceptional job of remembering Elliot. A few of the things we do to remember her are giving her gifts at Christmas, making her a Christmas stocking, and going on memory walks with other bereaved parents. Elliot continues to be part of our family. Three and a half years later, Elliot's parents now have two beautiful little girls. My daughter-in-law and I continue to participate in separate support groups, and I feel the need to support other grandparents who have experienced the loss of a grandchild.

Kathleen talks about miscarriage:

I have one grandson whom I adore. His mother, my daughter, wants another baby so badly. She has had five miscarriages. The first one was thought to be twins. I know it's not like losing a child after birth, but it has been and still is the saddest thing I've experienced in my life. I still get very weepy when I think of it and find it hard to deal with. How I wish I could help my daughter. This situation brings sadness to us all.

Bathsheeba's Son

Remember the story of King David and Bathsheeba? David saw Bathsheeba and wanted her. Even though she was already married, David sent her husband, Uriah, into battle and then had the troops withdraw, resulting in her husband's untimely death. David committed adultery and then got rid of his competition. God sent Nathan, a prophet, to tell David that because of what he had done, his son with Bathsheeba would die. David was inconsolable, as any parent would be. He fasted, wept, and prayed—but the child died.

"Then David got up from the ground. After he had washed, put on lotions and changed his clothes, he went into the house of the LORD and worshiped. Then he went to his own house, and at his request they served him food, and he ate. His attendants asked him, 'Why are you acting this way? While the child was alive, you fasted and wept, but now that the child is dead, you get up and eat!'" (2 Samuel 12:20–21).

David knew that the baby was now with God and that one day they would be reunited in Heaven. "He answered, 'While the child was still alive,

I fasted and wept. I thought, "Who knows? The LORD maybe gracious to me and let the child live." But now that he is dead, why should I go on fasting? Can I bring him back again? I will go to him, but he will not return to me'" (2 Samuel: 22–23).

What the Bible *doesn't* tell us is how Bathsheeba felt. Was Bathsheeba as strong as David? Were there relatives who comforted her and grieved with her? We will never know, but I'm willing to guess that her reaction was different from David's. I can't imagine a woman strong enough to not go through a period of grief after losing a child. Even though as Christians we have the assurance of Heaven, that doesn't stop the sadness we feel from the death of a loved one. Everyone I have ever known goes through some sort of grief process. For some, it lasts longer than for others.

During the course of my grandmother's lifetime, she lost her mother at age three and had no memory of her. Her father, Poppa Bear (my name for him), died when I was about eight years old. My mother, Grandma's only daughter, died at the age of fifty-one, and my mother's older brother (Grandma's oldest son) followed her in death the next year. Grandma Layne was exceptionally strong. Although she grieved, she kept on getting up every day, praising God, and attending church. She lived alone in a house that was next to ours until she had a stroke and moved in with us. I am convinced that she lived to be eighty-nine years old not because she had an easy life, but rather because of her strong faith. She held on tight to God's promises and kept living her life with strength and dignity.

There is no correct way to mourn. We all experience grief differently and deal with it one day at a time. In times of sorrow, there is an old hymn that reminds me of where to find comfort.

What a Friend We Have in Jesus
by Joseph M. Scriven

What a friend we have in Jesus,
All our sins and griefs to bear!
What a privilege to carry
Everything to God in prayer!
Oh, what peace we often forfeit,
Oh, what needless pain we bear,
All because we do not carry
Everything to God in prayer!
Have we trials and temptations?
Is there trouble anywhere?
We should never be discouraged—
Take it to the Lord in prayer.
Can we find a friend so faithful,

Who will all our sorrows share?
Jesus knows our every weakness;
Take it to the Lord in prayer.
Are we weak and heavy-laden,
Cumbered with a load of care?
Precious Savior, still our refuge—
Take it to the Lord in prayer.
Do thy friends despise, forsake thee?
Take it to the Lord in prayer!
In His arms He'll take and shield thee,
Thou wilt find a solace there.

God's Promises

"Weeping may last through the night,
but joy comes with the morning."
(Psalm 30:5, NLT)

"I will comfort you . . . as a mother
comforts her child." (Isaiah 66:13, NLT)

(continued)

"For the Lord has comforted his people and will have compassion on them in their suffering." (Isaiah 49:13, NLT)

"Give your burdens to the Lᴏʀᴅ, and he will take care of you." (Psalm 55:22, NLT)

"I will comfort those who mourn, bringing words of praise to their lips." (Isaiah 57:18–19, NLT)

"He will swallow up death forever! The Sovereign Lᴏʀᴅ will wipe away all tears." (Isaiah 25:8, NLT)

"Now let your unfailing love comfort me, just as you promised me, your servant." (Psalm 119:76, NLT)

"God himself will be with them [His people]. He will wipe every tear from their eyes, and there will be no more death or sorrow or crying or pain." (Revelation 21:3–4, NLT)

"When doubts filled my mind, your comfort gave me renewed hope and cheer." (Psalm 94:19, NLT)

"God is our merciful Father and the source of all comfort. He comforts us in all our troubles so that we can comfort others." (2 Corinthians 1:3–4, NLT)

A Grandmother's Prayer

Heavenly Father, when our hearts are hurting for our grandchildren and our children, we know you understand. Comfort us as only you can and remind us that even though weeping may last through the night, joy will come on that morning of glory when we come to be with you in Heaven. And when we see others grieving, help us to reach out to them and support them in any way we can. Amen.

Advice from Grandmothers

"My advice is to be there to listen—REALLY listen, and then you will know how to best help them move forward." —**Susan**

"Be very careful what you say to someone who is grieving. Your words can actually harm more than help." —**Betsy**

"Give yourself permission to grieve. Don't fight it. Take things one day at a time and pray, pray, pray." —**Samantha**

CHAPTER 9

The Physical Challenges of Being a Grandmother

All of us would like to be blessed with good health forever, but it just doesn't work that way. Many of us face health challenges that not only affect our daily lives; they can also change how and when we interact with our grandchildren.

My children were very young when my mother was diagnosed with terminal cancer. According to her oncologist, we knew she had about a year left to spend with us. Mom was determined to make the most of the time she had left. When she was physically able, she spent as much time as possible with her grandchildren.

As soon as summer vacation began, she insisted on taking my husband and I and her three grandchildren to Disneyland. We packed up all her medicines, rented a wheelchair, and spent a week visiting the parks. Somehow, she found the strength to get out of her wheelchair and took her grandchildren all the way through the Swiss Family Robinson tree house. We were all amazed!

That trip was around the first of June; Mom gained her angel wings around the end of July. I am convinced that the trip to Disney was her last gift to her grandchildren and that God had blessed her with just enough strength to endure that last vacation. I know there were days when she was in a lot of pain—but she never complained.

When we are faced with physical problems, we can and should be like Paul, who described his disability as a "thorn in my flesh." "Three times I pleaded with the Lord to take it away from me. But he said to me, 'My grace is sufficient for you, for my power is made perfect in weakness.' Therefore I will boast all the more gladly about my weaknesses, so that Christ's power may rest on me" (2 Corinthians 12:8–9).

No one knows what Paul's "thorn" was. There have been many guesses, but the Bible doesn't say. What Paul's story does tell us is that when we have a problem, even when we pray, sometimes we are going to get a "no" for an answer. But it is our attitude about how we handle a "no" from God that reveals our character. Our trust and obedience to His will is a huge part of living a faith-filled life.

Three Pieces of Advice for Physically Challenged Grandmothers

Becky Galli is a talented writer who became wheelchair bound at the age of thirty-eight. She's written a book about her experience called *Rethinking Possible: A Memoir of Resilience*, which chronicles her quest to live fully in the life she didn't plan.

She graciously agreed to share her thoughts about the challenges she faces as a wheelchair-bound grandmother. Becky writes:

1. Feel the loss.

"Sometimes I think we try to 'fix things' too soon as we slip into parent mode with our adult children. It's okay to feel the loss of unfulfilled dreams, or the anger of physical limitations, or the sadness of having to adjust ONE MORE TIME to the life you must live—not the one you had planned. You may not feel comfortable sharing those feelings with your children, but find someone you can trust and share what you are feeling."

2. Face reality and find humor when you can.

"When you've had enough of your 'pity party,' consider the evidence of the situation and face reality. Paralyzed by transverse myelitis, an inflammation of the spinal cord that affects one in a million, my abdominal muscles stopped working about two inches above my belly button. It is difficult for me to take both hands and put them together in the center of my body. When I try it, I wobble. Wobbling and newborns are not a good combination. That's a fact I needed to accept.

So, could I change a diaper? I thought about using my lap tray, but my legs are not stable. One leg spasm could easily send my lap tray tumbling; again, a fact. I shuddered when I envisioned it. But, if I'm honest, there was no great loss on that chore, right?"

3. Focus on what you still have, not what you've lost.

"Once you accept your reality, get creative and 'do what you can with what you've got.' After Blakely Faye was born, I realized I could hold her if I planted my elbows firmly on my armrests and tilted back my power wheelchair to stabilize my lap. As she grew, I found she could sit in my lap if she perched on my left knee and I used a football hold across her body. Soon I was driving her around and around our dining room table, singing, 'She'll be coming around that mountain.' She giggled with joy!

"And isn't that what it's about? Finding ways to share joy? Let love fuel your creativity, your search for possibilities. Despite physical limitations. Despite our circumstances. Despite all that we have lost, we can still find the joy in what we have if we take the time to accept what we know and rethink what's still possible."

Becky is one resilient grandmother. I admire her for her determination to be an involved grandparent to her grandchild, whom she obviously loves very much. I especially appreciate her words of wisdom on focusing on what you still have, not on what you have lost. That takes courage.

God's Promises

"Praise be to the God and Father of our Lord Jesus Christ, the Father of compassion and the God of all comfort, who comforts us in all our troubles, so that we can comfort those in any trouble with the comfort we ourselves receive from God."
(2 Corinthians 1:3–4)

"'He will wipe every tear from their eyes. There will be no more death' or mourning or crying or pain, for the old order of things has passed away."
(Revelations 21:4)

"For our light and momentary troubles are achieving for us an eternal glory that far outweighs them all. So we fix our eyes not on what is seen, but on

what is unseen, since what is seen
is temporary, but what is unseen is
eternal." (2 Corinthians 4:17–18)

"I consider that our present sufferings
are not worth comparing with the
glory that will be revealed in us."
(Romans 8:18)

A Grandmother's Prayer

Heavenly Father, when we are hurting, and illness and pain keep us from doing the things we would like to do with our grandchildren, help us remember that these sufferings will not compare to the glory you have created for us. Heaven will be a wonderful place where you will wipe away every tear. Keep us focused on you until we reach that place where there will be no more mourning or crying or pain. Amen.

Advice from Grandmothers

"I have mobility issues, as well as chronic pain. I had gastric sleeve surgery last year. My grandchildren know I am not able to keep up all the time, but because they are older it's easier for them to understand. They remind me of what I am allowed and not allowed to do. I have had to find alternative ways to be in their lives. We go to movies and hang out together. We have special restaurants we visit (each grandchild has their own favorite). My advice is that any grandma with physical limitations can still schedule special one-on-one time with each grandchild and organize a special visit or activity just for them." —**Donna**

"I have chronic fibromyalgia, MS, and PTSD. When I am in a bad pain event, I tell my grandchildren that I am hurting and we lie on my bed and watch movies. My fourteen- and eight-year-old have been taught that Grandma has diseases, and I have had to use my wheelchair and walker and cane at times. But nothing will stop my love for them. On my good days, I make up for the bad days!" —**Kimmie**

"I am a grandparent who has been diagnosed with three pain diseases. I feel like I fall far short in the grandparent department. Frequently, my body is yelling 'lie down' while my family is yelling 'where are you?' I am in a constant struggle with which one to answer. Through patience and time, my grandchildren have come to understand my limitations. I rely on my husband to take my place. He is a great 'Pappaw.' Rarely is he not present when asked to watch the grands. I read to my grandchildren, alternating between books that I let them choose. They pick from books that I used to read to their dad, which makes it even more meaningful. When their other grandmother approached them to read a book, my grandson replied, 'That's something Mammie does.' It makes me feel honored and blessed that he associates reading with Mammie-time. Now that each grandchild is older, we do crafts, watch movies, or play simple card

(continued)

games, board games, or Jenga—anything that keeps me seated. Occasionally, when I'm able, we play corn hole and ball in the backyard. Another thing grandmothers with physical challenges have to do is concentrate on the positive instead of the negative. When I can give 100 percent, I do. When I cannot, I do what I can. Sometimes I have to say 'no' to their requests. When I do, they are learning patience and understanding, something much needed in the world today." —**Theresa**

"I'm quite deaf and have hearing aids for both ears. It can be embarrassing and humorous when we are looking after our three-year-old grandson! He gets frustrated when I don't hear or understand him. Recently, he was at our house and I was giving him a bath. I poured water over his throat, like he'd told me to. Next, it turned out he was saying it was choking him, though I thought he was saying he wanted some toast! Luckily his grandad was there to interpret!" —**Kathleen**

"My physical challenges are numerous. I'm always exhausted and barely able to function most days because of my chronic fatigue and the pain from fibromyalgia and arthritis. Summers are the hardest because my kids depend on me to babysit since the grandchildren are out of school. I have six wonderful grandbabies and another one arriving in November. It breaks my heart that I can't get up and interact and play with them like I want to. They have all come to realize that Nana can't do a lot of things. I push myself to the point of making myself sick sometimes to be able to go out and enjoy a day or weekend with them. My only advice is to just do what you can and make the most of those precious moments with your grandbabies. They will love you regardless of what you can or can't do." —Teresa

CHAPTER 10

Multi-Generational Families under the Same Roof

I got in the shower this morning and stepped over two dolls and a plastic toy boat. The grandchildren showered in my bathroom last night. I laughed and thought about the joy of having two of my grandchildren living in our house. Their parents, my daughter and son-in-law, live with us, as well as another son who is engaged to be married.

As the parents of five children, we have had each of them move back home at one time or another for various reasons. When people ask me how we like having a house full of people at this stage of our lives, I tell them the truth: we love it. We wouldn't have had five kids if we didn't love children. Having little ones in the house again after our children are all grown up is so much fun!

Multigenerational households like ours are on the rise in America. In 2016, a record 64 million people, or 20 percent of the US population, lived with multiple generations under one roof, according to a new Pew Research Center analysis of census data. In Canada, the 2016 census showed a 37.5 percent increase in the number of multigenerational households since 2001. Multigenerational homes are also common in other cultures, including in Hispanic and Asian families.

Remember the popular television show *The Waltons* that ran from 1971 to 1981? It was the story of a large family who all lived in the same house during the Great Depression. Each episode ended with family members calling out to each other and saying goodnight. I loved the show, and the concept of many people living together in one house never seemed unusual to me. This might in part be because my mother grew up in a house with her brothers, her parents, and her grandmother; then years later after my parents had both died, my grandmother came to live with my husband and I and our five children. Grandma Layne seemed to enjoy the noise and chaos of a busy family, and we cherished having her with us. She loved feeling like she was helping out—one of her favorite jobs was folding laundry, which she often did while sitting and watching television. One day as she was folding laundry, my teenage daughter's underwear happened to be in the basket. Watching her try to figure out how to fold a tiny undergarment that looked like it was held together with dental floss is a memory I will treasure forever!

My friend Donna also has a full house. Donna says, "My thirty-one-year-old daughter and her two children, ages nine and three, moved in with us after her relationship with the children's father broke up due to drugs, alcohol, and abuse. They showed up with just the clothes on their backs. She had been a stay-at-home mother with no job or source of income and was scared and traumatized by what she'd went through. So were the children. It has been a year since they moved in. They are all much better, my daughter is working, and the kids are now thriving. But it has been an adjustment to open up my 'empty nest,' which I *loved*, to welcome a whole other family and all that brings with it."

Lessons Learned

Donna shares some of the lessons she learned from having her daughter and grandchildren live with her. Her thoughts, I believe, will benefit others who may find themselves suddenly no longer living in an empty nest.

Here is her advice:

1. The way your child raises their children is different than the way you raised yours.
"My grandchildren are perfect! But I do have a few rules that I insist on at my house. All food is eaten at the table. Don't throw balls in the house or jump on the furniture.

"Other than that, I am not their mother. She is responsible for their discipline and I don't comment on how she brings them up or suggest things to her. Okay, maybe I have a time or two, but I really try to refrain from that."

2. Don't jump in to solve all their problems.
"Sometimes your children come home and are in pain, either through their own doing or maybe through no fault of their own. You are their mom, so you want to do anything you can, whatever it costs, to fix it all. And you may need to do some of that.

"Just don't have a knee-jerk reaction and try to take care of all their problems immediately. If their issues are not time-sensitive, you don't have to do something *today*; give them time to figure it out.

"The truth is, your children really don't need Mommy and Daddy solving all of their problems—even though they may act like they want it. It's not good for them. Someday, we won't be here to save or help them, so they have to learn strategies to help themselves. Plus, when they do come home to live, they often come with their tail between their legs. Their self-confidence is shot. Being able to solve a few problems themselves really helps their self-esteem and does wonders in eventually moving them toward the path to independence."

3. Don't be on call 24 hours a day.

"Don't make yourself available at every hour to give your children a ride, take care of their kids, etc. Yes, you can do any of those things you want. But they need to ask, and it needs to fit in with your schedule.

"It is so easy, especially with your life experience and your own habits in raising kids, to predetermine what is needed and find a way to manage it for them before they even have a chance to ask. I often thought things like, 'Amy has a doctor's appointment and needs someone to watch this kids, so I'll stay home and do it,' before I was even asked. I was assuming what needed to be done and taking it upon myself to do it. Wait to be asked to help and don't plan your days around them, or they will become too dependent on you. Remember: you want them to be able to function independently of you so that when the time comes, they will be able to do things on their own.

4. Don't give up your own life.

"When someone you love is in crisis, it's natural to drop everything to help them. But doing that in the long term is not good for you, and it's not good for them. I found myself getting very resentful when I felt that I had to give everything up that I loved about my empty-nester life to fill in the gaps in my adult child's life. And my seething resentment was making me sick and doing nothing for my relationship with my daughter.

"I need to always remind myself that this is a season. A season when my daughter has to live with us. I don't know how long it will last, and I can't control it. But in the big picture, having a good relationship with her over the long haul is the objective."

Donna's wise advice is indeed very valuable for multigenerational families under one roof. To that, I will add a fifth point:

5. Respect each other's space.

When our daughter and son-in-law moved in with their two children, we converted a room into a toy room upstairs, which helps keep the downstairs area less cluttered. The toys have a way of migrating downstairs, but they eventually go back where they belong. My daughter's family lives in the basement and we are respectful of their privacy. I always knock before I go down and I do my best to treat the basement as if it's a separate house. We enjoy cooking together and often share meal preparation and mealtime, but it really helps if everyone has a private place (no matter how small) they can call their own. Respect each other's space.

God's Promises

God reminds us that love never fails! If families focus on their love for one another, there is no reason they can't live together if they choose too.

(continued)

"Love must be sincere. Hate what is evil; cling to what is good. Be devoted to one another in love. Honor one another above yourselves." (Romans 12:9–10)

A Grandmother's Prayer

Lord, help us remember your patience with us, and help us have that same attitude toward our families. We know that our patience with others may wear thin when we are weary and that there's the danger we will say something we shouldn't. Help us to be in control of our tongues and always choose our words carefully. We love our family members and know that a soft answer turns away wrath; but grievous words stir up anger. Help us to always be gentle and kind when dealing with whatever problems a multigenerational household may face. Amen.

Advice from Grandmothers

"We live in El Paso, Texas, with my mom, my daughter, and her son and daughter. I left my job in San Diego to live with my daughter last year when she developed health problems related to Ehlers-Danlos syndrome. I bought a five-bedroom duplex and we constructed a passageway so the whole house is connected. My favorite thing is having my family in one spot; I love spending time with them. My least favorite thing about this arrangement is the occasions when I need some time alone. (Rare, but necessary.) I would recommend to any family thinking about moving in together that everyone should really like each other and get along. I would also recommend that household duties are assigned so no one person is doing more than their fair share. Also, a weekly round table is great to discuss anything and everything. I love being with my mother and my grandbabies at the same time!" —Michelle

Final Thoughts

When I was a little girl, I hated shots and going to the doctor. Every time I had an appointment, I would question my mother, demanding to know whether or not I was going to get a shot.

Before one particular visit, she had promised me that there were no vaccinations scheduled. Unfortunately, when we arrived, the doctor looked at my chart and informed us that I was in fact overdue for a vaccination. My mother asked if we could postpone it, but for whatever reason they insisted I get it that day.

I didn't make things easy for my mother or the nurse. I cried and screamed, "You lied to me!" at the top of my lungs.

My mother felt terrible about her mistake and

never made promises again concerning doctor's visits. Even though she didn't intentionally break a promise, she still broke one.

God doesn't break promises. Ever.

"Not one of all the LORD's good promises
to Israel failed; every one was fulfilled."
(Joshua 21:45)

When I became the mother of three young children, I thought my life couldn't get much crazier. Then we had twins. Those years are literally a blur. The photographs of me during those moments show someone who is too skinny, very tired, and who looks like she could use a good night's sleep and a haircut. But there was never time or money for me to do everything I thought I needed to do. I don't think I sat down for more than five minutes at a time after 1981. They were crazy, busy years; but they were also some of the best years of my life. I wish I had prayed more and worried less. I was definitely a Martha instead of a Mary when it came to worrying about what was really important.

Now that I'm a grandparent, I am finally able to live in the moment without worrying about things like whether all five kids had brushed their teeth before bedtime. That may sound trivial, but one of my sons actually thanked me for it—once, when I went away for a weekend, his dad forgot to make him brush his teeth!

All those essential child-caring jobs now belong to my children. I'm free to spoil, play, and pamper. When the grandchildren spend the night, I still make them brush their teeth of course—old habits die hard! Plus, I don't want the little darlings to get cavities.

With my grandchildren, I am finally at the stage in my life where I do pray more and worry less. I trust their parents to make the best decisions they can regarding child-rearing, and I wait for them to ask me for help before I share my opinions.

I'm Nana, not Mom.

Being a grandmother is a privilege and honor that not every woman gets to experience. I'm so thankful for this, but I also feel a responsibility to my grandchildren that I didn't expect. I think about my mother and my Grandma Layne and wonder if I can fill their shoes. Can I live my life as well as they did theirs? Will my progeny remember me as a faith-filled grandmother who tried her best to follow in the footsteps of Jesus? Do other grandmothers think about how they can be the best example to their grands?

I believe this book is evidence that they do. We

want to do right by our grandchildren; we want them to be prepared to face a world that is quick to judge and often too eager to disagree. How do we help build their faith and plant those seeds of God's word in their hearts? Especially when some of us live far away or don't see them as often as we would like? What if, in the case of some grandmothers, we don't see them at all?

I think the answer is we do it in the same way my Grandmother Layne did. By holding on to God's promises. By going to Him daily in prayer. By listening to other grandmothers who have been there and done that; by hearing their practical advice and, most important, preaching the best possible sermon we can with how we live our lives.

Blessings to you and your families. May the good Lord hold you and your family always in the palm of his hand.

—Teresa Kindred

Acknowledgments

To Bill, my husband and best friend. You are my man of character, and, like the song says, "I love you forever and ever . . . Amen!"

To Nick, Rachel, Justin, Russell, and Grant. God couldn't have given your Dad and I a greater earthly gift than each of you and your families. We are blessed!

To my precious grandchildren, Abby, Chandler, Kennedy, Brynlee, Knox, and Ana, you bring such joy to our lives, and we love you to infinity and beyond!

And finally, to the grandmothers and friends who shared their wisdom and the stories of their hearts to help me write this book . . . thank you. This is "our" book, and I truly appreciate each and every one of my NanaHood friends.